CALLED

TO

MANHOOD

Table of Contents

Table of Contents

Works Cited

Barna. (2019). *spiritually vibrant household.* Retrieved from Barna: https://www.barna.com/research/spiritually-vibrant-household/

Barna. (2024, October). *Beyond the Porn Phenomenon.* Retrieved from Barna.com: https://www.barna.com/trends/over-half-of-practicing-christians-admit-they-use-pornography/

Burows, R. D. (2022, July 17). *Robb-Elementary-Investigative-Committee-Report-update.* Retrieved from Texas House: https://www.house.texas.gov/pdfs/committees/reports/interim/87interim/Robb-Elementary-Investigative-Committee-Report-update.pdf

Earls, A. (2024). *Small Groups Remain Key Aspect of Churches' Discipleship Ministry.* Retrieved from Lifeway Research: https://research.lifeway.com/2024/09/12/small-groups-remain-key-aspect-of-churches-discipleship-ministry/

Kramer, S. (2019, December). *U.S. has world's highest rate of children living in single-parent households.* Retrieved from Pew Research: https://www.pewresearch.org/short-reads/2019/12/12/u-s-children-more-likely-than-children-in-other-countries-to-live-with-just-one-parent/

Lippold MA, M. S. (2015). *Day-to-day inconsistency in parental knowledge.* Retrieved from The Journal of Adolescent Health: https://pmc.ncbi.nlm.nih.gov/articles/PMC4338414/

Zammit, I. &. (2023). *A systematic review of the association between religiousness and children's prosociality.* Retrieved from Religion, Brain & Behavior: https://doi.org/10.1080/2153599X.2022.2131892

About the Author

At fifty-seven, a husband and father of three daughters stands as a witness of God's relentless grace. His story began, as many do, in the house of God. He was the grandson of a Pentecostal pastor, raised in pews where hymns were sung, Bibles were read, and prayers stretched long into the night.

The sanctuary was his first classroom. There he learned to make music, his young fingers discovering chords on the church piano. There he first heard that God was holy, loving, and near. Yet it was also in that sacred space that the brokenness of a fallen world crept in, planting seeds of doubt and disillusion.

Abuse, divorce, and deception each left their mark. The faith that had seemed unshakable in childhood began to crack under wounds left unhealed.

By his teenage years, James was listening to a darker voice. The whisper grew louder with time: "God is distant. The church is a farce. You are on your own." Lies once entertained hardened into convictions. The boy raised in the sanctuary became a young man who declared in defiance that God was dead to him.

James embraced atheism with zeal. He wasn't merely skeptical; he became an opponent of believers. Like Saul before Damascus, he used his intellect as a weapon. He debated Christians wherever he found them. He dismantled arguments with sharp logic and a wounded heart.

His passion for justice, though sincere, was misplaced. He wanted to fight corruption, to expose hypocrisy, to strike against institutions he believed were built on lies. That passion led him into dark alliances, including with the hacking collective Anonymous.

Behind the screen and the thrill of rebellion, James thought he was fighting for truth. In time, he saw he was running from the Author of truth.

Two broken marriages followed. Years of addiction and self-loathing pulled him deeper. Nights blurred into days, and days into years, as despair hollowed him out.

He carried anger as armor, wielded sarcasm as a shield, and wore skepticism as a crown. On the surface he appeared sharp, tough, and unbothered. Inside he was falling apart. Hope felt not only distant but extinguished.

But God. Two words that rewrite every story. The same Jesus who met Saul on the Damascus Road, blinding him with light and truth, was not finished with James. In his darkest hour, the grace of God broke through like a floodlight in a cave.

It was no slow persuasion. There was no gentle nudge back to religion. It was a divine confrontation with truth. An undeniable encounter with the living Christ. Lies that had ruled his heart for decades crumbled in a moment. The love of Jesus pierced pride, shame, and deception. The Spirit of God reached into his abyss and called him back to life.

Grace gave him more than rescue. It gave him a future. God placed him in a spiritual family and blessed him with a wife whose faith rekindled his own. He entrusted him with the joy of fatherhood. The laughter of three daughters proved that God could rebuild what sin tried to destroy. Even these blessings were not the end. They prepared him for something great: a calling.

James began to see that his past was not wasted. The wounds that once enslaved him became open doors for ministry. He began to lead men out of the same shadows he once knew so well: addiction, anger, and despair.

He became a group leader in Re:Generation, a Christ-centered recovery ministry. He pursued seminary training with the same zeal he once used to attack the faith. He became a licensed Mental Health Coach, using both professional tools and biblical wisdom to counsel the hurting.

He took on leadership not to build a platform but to build people. His story showed that God does not call the flawless but redeems the broken.

Like Paul, who once hunted Christians and later shepherded churches, James now leverages his past not as a source of shame but as a foundation for the gospel.

His testimony is no longer about how far a man can fall, but how deep God's mercy can reach. Every part of his journey is tied to one mission. To guide men from darkness into the light of Christ.

Today, James's heartbeat is simple to reveal to other men what he himself searched for in vain, until grace found him. To be fully known, fully forgiven, and fully loved by God. That's the joy, the anchor.

The legacy he seeks now is not rebellion but redemption.

CALLED TO MANHOOD

You can follow James' Blog and find out more about his ministry
at jamesdornan.com

Dedication

My story begins with grace. I must first honor the person God used to bring me back to Him, my wife

This work is dedicated to her, because she has been a steady presence through the darkest valleys and the brightest mountaintops.

"Her life has taught me more than sermons. Her forgiveness showed me Christ's mercy. Her faithfulness reminded me of His love.

This book explores manhood, marriage, fatherhood, and grace. Before I wrote these words, I saw them lived out in my wife. She believed God was not finished with me, and she chose to stand in the gap until I believed it too.

I pray that what follows will not simply be words on a page but living encouragement to you. My hope is that you will see through my story and through the timeless truth of Scripture, that God is still in the business of restoring what is broken. And that, like me, you will be reminded that redemption often begins with one faithful person who refuses to give up.

For me, it was my wife. For you, my prayer is that these pages point you to hope in Christ.

My own journey of brokenness and restoration has shaped what follows. These pages are not theory but lived truth.

The Call to Biblical Manhood

"Be watchful, stand firm in the faith, act like men, be strong. Let all that you do be done in love." 1 Corinthians 16:13–14

At fifteen, my parents divorced. The memory is sharp, carved into my soul. One day life felt whole. The next, it was shattered. I remember the silence more than the shouting. The emptiness more than the arguments.

Everything I was sure of collapsed. The people who had taught me everything suddenly revealed that the life we lived together was not what it seemed. Trust fractured, and with it the framework I had built my world upon.

In those years I carried confusion like a shadow. I questioned what was real. I questioned what could be trusted. I asked what it meant to be a man when the example I needed most was gone.

Anger grew in the cracks of my heart. Yet a hunger also grew. A hunger for something solid. Something that would not shift beneath my feet. I did not know it then, but God was planting the first seeds of a truth I would later learn. Earthly fathers may fail. The Father in heaven does not abandon His sons.

This struck me at the core in a mighty way. If my parents' love was not real, if they could walk away, then what else they taught me was not real either.

The questions came like a flood. If their promises could be broken, how could I trust any promise at all? And if their love could fail, what about God's? Would He leave me too? Was He even real?

A Global Crisis of Manhood

My broken home was one story, but it reflects a wider fracture in how a generation understands manhood.

Across the world, a crisis of identity is unfolding.

We see the crisis everywhere. A boy turns to YouTube for lessons his father never gave. Churches fall quiet where men once prayed and led.

The Four Pillars of Biblical Manhood

When God pulled me out of that valley of brokenness, He did more than rescue me. He rebuilt me. Every lesson rested on four unshakable pillars that became the foundation of my life. These same pillars will guide our journey in this book.

Identity

For years, I built my worth on success, relationships, reputation, and control. None endured. In Christ, I found identity is not achieved. It is received as a gift.

Purpose

Before Christ, my purpose centered on myself: comfort, security, proving my worth. When God stepped in, He redefined everything. I was created for His glory, not my own. My purpose became one of representing His kingdom, not building my own.

Leadership

I once thought leadership was about position. God showed me it is measured by service and sacrifice. Leading my family required humility, protection, and guidance, not control.

True leadership is not a title but a cross to bear.

Spiritual Warfare

In my old life, I thought my struggles were only circumstantial: bad luck, poor timing, or the fault of others. I did not realize I was in a spiritual war.

These four pillars are not abstract. They are the beams God used to rebuild my life, the structure that turned collapse into restoration. Without them, a man drifts, unsettled by the shifting voices around him. With them, he stands firm, not in his own strength but in Christ.

This book will make the pillars clear. It will show you how to strengthen them. It will prepare you for the spiritual fight.

The Confusion

Society sends mixed messages. Some celebrate power without responsibility. Others call masculinity unnecessary or even harmful. Caught between the two, many men become what James 1:8 calls "a double-minded man, unstable in all his ways."

God has not left us guessing. He has spoken clearly about who we are and why we exist. We are not accidents of biology or products of culture. We are image-bearers of the living God, created to reflect His glory in how we live, love, work, and lead.

Our worth is not earned by money, strength, or reputation. It is given through adoption in Christ. We are no longer strangers but sons.

This changes everything. The world urges men to prove themselves. The gospel declares our identity is a gift from God, not a reward for effort

When a man rests in that truth, he is freed from chasing approval. He becomes equipped to give what his family and world most need: a steady reflection of the Father's heart.

My Own Wandering

For years, I resisted the truth. With no compass for godly manhood, I crowned myself king of a fragile kingdom. My morality bent to desire. My ambition covered an empty soul. Outwardly, I looked fine, like a freshly painted house. Beneath the surface, the boards were soft and rotting.

I chased success, comfort, and control as if they were lifeboats in a storm. Ambition became my anthem. Screens became my firelight. Applause became my daily bread. None delivered the peace they promised. They provided only noise. It grew louder until it drowned out the still, small voice of God.

Inside, my soul was hollow. An empty room where only my echo answered back. I wore confidence like a mask. Behind it, my relationships were paper-thin. My integrity was fractured. My heart was like a restless wanderer without a home.

Like the people in the time of Judges, I lived by my own truth:

"IN THOSE DAYS THERE WAS NO KING IN ISRAEL. EVERYONE DID
WHAT WAS RIGHT IN HIS OWN EYES"
JUDGES 21:25.

That verse became a mirror to my soul, showing me what I did not want to see. I was kingless, as were countless other men I knew.

The Struggle

Biblical manhood is often misunderstood. Scripture told us to expect this. The question is how we live with clarity and grace.

Scripture warns that good gifts can be distorted. Strength and integrity are sometimes recast as dangerous. God's design remains good.

This distortion is not manhood. It is sin disguised. Arrogance that feeds the self, violence that harms, and cowardice that abandons responsibility are not fruits of manhood. They are the scars of a fallen world.

In an age that misunderstands and fears masculinity, we must recover its biblical meaning. God created manhood not to oppress but to bless. Not to dominate but to serve.

True masculinity rests in a calling rooted in God's image. It is embracing God-given strength and using it for His glory and the good of others

It protects the vulnerable, as Boaz did for Ruth. It leads with integrity, as Nehemiah did while rebuilding Jerusalem's walls. It serves with humility, as Christ did when He washed His disciples' feet.

God's Design

God has not left family to caricatures. His Word calls men to lead with humility, strength, and sacrificial love.

Joseph protected Mary and the infant Christ from Herod's violence. Nehemiah defended Jerusalem with a trowel in one hand and a sword in the other. Joseph in Egypt resisted temptation, not out of fear but from reverence for God.

Men as the Leader

When men lead their families, it does not demean women. It honors God's design. Paul shows that headship means sacrificial love. Husbands are to lay down their lives as Christ did for the church.

That kind of leadership is not tyranny. It is servant-leadership. It dignifies, protects, and nurtures. It seeks the flourishing of others, even at personal cost. Far from being a threat to women, biblical manhood, when lived rightly, becomes a shield of honor and a source of blessing.

To affirm that God created male and female is not an act of hate. It is an affirmation of reality.

When male and female are denied, confusion follows. Science affirms the reality, and Scripture affirms the beauty, of God's design.

These truths may be unpopular. They are not new or oppressive. They are ancient, tested, and life-giving. Biblical manhood is not a cultural construct that can be deconstructed at will. It is God's design for flourishing. Rejecting it does not bring freedom. It leaves families without direction and generations without an anchor.

What's at Stake

For Christian men, the stakes could not be higher. This is not only about schools or curricula. It is about guarding the kingdoms God has placed in our care. Our homes and children stand at the front lines. We must anchor them in the unshakable Word of God.

God designed the home for nurture. When that design is redefined, families fracture, men drift, and responsibility weakens.

For men, husbands, fathers, and leaders, this moment calls for vigilance. It calls us to reclaim our God-given role as protectors and shepherds of the next generation. We cannot hand over responsibility to systems that deny the Author of truth. Instead, we must anchor our homes, our communities, and our children in the unshakable Word of God.

The decline of a society that rejects its Creator is described clearly in Romans.

"THEY EXCHANGED THE TRUTH ABOUT GOD FOR A LIE AND
WORSHIPED AND SERVED CREATED THINGS RATHER THAN THE
CREATOR"
ROMANS 1:25

This warning is not abstract. It is unfolding before our eyes. We see a reversal of values where the sacred is dismissed and the profane is elevated.

Marriage is often dismissed, while shifting ideas of self are praised as progress. Yet Scripture offers a vision that brings stability and hope.

Faith is often sidelined in public spaces, while money, fame, and self-expression are lifted up as virtues. These are not isolated trends. They are signs of a culture that has traded God's truth for lies.

The same contrast appears in relationships and responsibility. Choices that leave behind broken homes and wounded children are called courageous. The destruction is ignored while the rebellion is celebrated.

The Message

The cultural message is often clear. Rebellion is celebrated while righteousness is dismissed or ignored. This reversal twists freedom and weakens the foundations of families and communities.

The battle for manhood is not just a social debate. It is a spiritual struggle. The soul of a generation is at stake. The future of families and faith hangs in the balance.

Marriage is often minimized. Fatherhood overlooked. Manhood confused. Yet the biblical vision still convicts and stands firm.

Answering the Call

We live in a time when the very definition of manhood is questioned. Culture tells men to be passive and silent or domineering and selfish. Biblical manhood charts a different path. It is anchored in Christ, rooted in truth, and lived out in love.

This is not about reclaiming a nostalgic picture of masculinity. It is about rediscovering God's design and living it with courage.

13

The pressures are often subtle, eroding over time. Strength, courage, protection, and leadership are sometimes dismissed as unnecessary or even harmful.

When men lose sight of who they are, they drift from purpose. The damage is quiet but real. A generation grows up doubting its worth and shrinking from truth.

God has not left us without help. He has given us His Word as a blueprint. He has given us His Spirit as our power. He has given us His Son as our example. If we rest in who we are in Christ, embrace our purpose, lead with humility, and walk with courage, we can resist the darkness.

This book is not abstract. It is a guide for becoming the man God designed you to be, no matter how strong the challenges feel.

My prayer is that as you read, you will not only be stirred but also shaped. That you will rise as a man who knows who he is in Christ, why he was created, and what it means to walk in true biblical manhood.

This is not a call to perfection. It is a call to purpose. Not to cultural trends, but to eternal truth. May you read with an open heart, ready to be challenged, equipped, and transformed for the battles that matter most.

Reflection

- Name one area where you've stayed silent and commit to speaking truth with courage.

- Remove one distraction that dulls your vigilance and replace it with time in prayer or the Word.

- Take one intentional step to model redeemed masculinity in your family, church, or community.

- Reach out to one brother in Christ to begin building mutual accountability and encouragement.

Prayer

Lord, we thank You that You are not silent or absent. You are the God who sees, who speaks, and who leads. Yet we confess, Father, that we have often fallen short. We were silent when we should have spoken, retreated when we should have stood firm, and compromised when we should have been courageous. Give us courage to resist the lies of our culture and boldness to stand for what is right, even when it costs us. Raise us up as protectors, providers, and spiritual leaders in our homes, churches, and communities. Unite us as brothers, sharpen us as men, and send us out as servants and warriors for Your kingdom. In Jesus' mighty name we pray, Amen.

Created with Purpose

"Then God said, 'Let us make man in our image, after our likeness...'", Genesis 1:26

Before a man becomes a husband, father, or leader, he must know this: he is not an accident.

His life is not the result of meaningless forces, blind chance, or cosmic indifference. Scripture affirms that he was created, intentionally, intricately, and lovingly, by the hands of a purposeful God.

This truth is the bedrock of biblical manhood. Without it, a man is left wandering. He chases his image in his career, his possessions, or the fleeting approval of others.

He may climb ladders, collect accolades, and appear successful in the eyes of the world. Yet deep down, he remains restless and insecure.

When this truth takes root, everything changes. He no longer lives to prove himself. He rests in what his Creator has already spoken. His worth is fixed, grounded in God's Word..

A life anchored in Christ is not defined by the applause of men but secured by the declaration of God Himself.

Man as Divine Design

Genesis 1–2 presents mankind not as an incidental development in nature but as the pinnacle of God's creative work:

"THEN THE LORD GOD FORMED THE MAN OF DUST FROM THE GROUND AND BREATHED INTO HIS NOSTRILS THE BREATH OF LIFE,

The Hebrew word for "formed" (*yatsar*) conveys the image of a potter carefully shaping clay, deliberate, intentional, and personal. Unlike the rest of creation, which God brought into being by His word, man was shaped by His hand.

The picture is one of divine intimacy: the Creator stooping low, fashioning humanity with precision, and then imparting His very breath. Man is not only animated matter, but a living being bearing the imprint of God's personal touch.

This act of creation establishes more than biological life, it bestows meaning, dignity, and divine intent. To be created in the image of God is to bear His likeness in character, authority, and relational capacity. It is to carry within our souls a reflection of His nature and to be entrusted with His mission on the earth.

Every man, regardless of age or background, bears the image of the Creator. That mark cannot be erased by sin or redefined by culture. It is sacred and secure.

The Competing Story

We see the fruit of that worldview all around us. When men believe they are nothing more than evolved animals, they begin to live like it. Relationships become transactional. Commitments dissolve when they no longer benefit the self. Pleasure becomes the highest good. In such a world, a man is defined not by eternal purpose but by temporary appetite, chasing satisfaction in wealth, lust, dominance, or distraction.

This truth gives weight to morality, permanence to love, and eternal meaning to small acts of faithfulness. A man's worth is not up for debate. It is fixed in God's decree.

Until a man embraces this truth, he will live restless, searching for meaning in achievements or applause. But once he knows he is created, called, and loved, his life finds clarity and direction.

Furthermore, the moral, intellectual, and spiritual capacities of humanity resist reduction to evolutionary explanation. We create art not only for survival, but to celebrate beauty. We mourn the dead, honor the elderly, and risk our lives for the vulnerable, acts that are difficult to explain in a purely survivalist framework.

Our longing for justice, our capacity for worship, and our ache for eternity are not evolutionary accidents; they are divine fingerprints, reminders that we are more than matter, we are image-bearers.

Here the stakes are not simply biological, they are theological.

If death is treated as the natural engine of progress, then it is no longer the enemy Christ came to conquer. If humanity progressively emerged without a historical Adam, then there was no literal fall, no inherited sin, and no need for a Second Adam to restore what was lost.

A purely evolutionary framework is not solely a scientific theory. It is a theological challenge that strikes at the heart of redemption. Without creation, there is no fall. Without the fall, there is no cross. Without the cross, there is no hope.

In a world chasing identity, the image of God is our anchor. It reminds us we are known, seen, and loved. Our worth is not earned. We were created with purpose.

The Carpenter's Bench

When I was a kid, my grandfather handed me a rough piece of wood and pointed to his old carpenter's bench. "Make something," he said with a smile. I stared at the cracked plank, not sure what to do. I tried carving, sanding, hammering nails, but all I managed was a mess of splinters and sawdust.

After watching me struggle, my grandfather walked over, took the same piece of wood, and in a matter of minutes shaped it into a simple, sturdy stool.

I remember asking him, "How did you know it could be that?" He chuckled and said, "The wood always had a purpose. I just followed it."

That moment stayed with me. What looked random and unusable in my hands had meaning in his. The stool was not an accident of guesswork. It was the result of design, guided by someone who knew what he was doing.

Like that wood, our purpose is built into us from the start. Only the Creator knows the grain of our soul, the shape of our calling, and the life we were made to live.

Without Him, we may spend years splintering ourselves against false identities and chasing approval. But in His hands, we become what we were always meant to be: crafted, steady, and useful for His glory.

Gods Vision for Manhood

God's Word speaks with unshakable clarity. Man was created by God and for God, designed to reflect His image, and entrusted with dignity, responsibility, and purpose.

Biblical manhood is active, engaged, and intentional, not defined by brute strength or social status, but by purpose and presence. A godly man serves, protects, and leads because he knows who he is and whose he is.

When Men Are Absent

The tragedy at Robb Elementary School in Uvalde, Texas, in 2022 agonizingly illustrated the cost of passivity. Law enforcement officers waited outside for over an hour while a gunman slaughtered children *(official Texas House report 2022)*. The failure to act at a moment of crisis costs lives, a modern echo of passivity. (Burows, 2022)

Contrast that with the actions of school caretaker Fousseynou Cissé who rescued six people, including four children, from a burning apartment building. Despite smoke filling the room, he braved standing on a sixth-floor ledge to reach those trapped. He passed a 1-month-old baby and a 1-year-old through a window to safety and continued rescuing two other children and two adults.

God calls men to be protectors, providers and cultivators. When these roles are abandoned, destruction follows.

Reflection

- Identify the cultural lies about manhood that have shaped your thinking and replace them with the truth of Scripture.

- Confess the areas where you have been silent or passive and ask God for courage to act.

- Commit to strengthening one biblical role, Protector, Provider, or Cultivator, that needs the most growth in your life.

- Decide on one specific change you will make this week to reflect God's image in your home.

Prayer

Father, thank You that I am fearfully and wonderfully made in Your image. I repent of the times I have been passive or self-centered. Teach me to walk in the fullness of my calling as a man created for Your glory. Empower me to protect, provide, and cultivate all You have entrusted to me. Let my life reflect Your Son, the perfect man. In Jesus' name, Amen.

Redeemed for Leadership

"Therefore, just as sin came into the world through one man, and death through sin... much more have the grace of God and the free gift by the grace of that one man Jesus Christ abounded for many." ,
Romans 5:12, 15

God formed Adam with purpose. From the first moment, He gave him a mission. Lead. Cultivate. Protect. Walk closely with the Creator. Genesis tells this story:

> "THE LORD GOD TOOK THE MAN AND PUT HIM IN THE GARDEN OF EDEN TO WORK IT AND KEEP IT."
> GENESIS 2:15

The language of Genesis is precise. "Work" (abad) means to serve with diligence. "Keep" (shamar) means to guard and protect. Adam was not a bystander in paradise. He was called to steward. He was called to defend. He was called to serve his Creator. His life was shaped to mirror God's own character.

This pattern defines true masculinity. Adam was given authority, but it was the authority to cultivate, not dominate. His strength was given to serve, not to grasp. This is the foundation of manhood. A man's strength, creativity, intellect, and voice are sacred trusts. They are to be used as blessings. They are to be used for righteousness. They are to reflect God's image in the world.

The Tragedy of Silence

In 2023, a respected pastor came under fire, not for scandal in the usual sense, but for enabling toxicity in his ministry through silence.

Though he had the authority to confront abuse and excess, he chose passivity. He feared conflict more than compromise.

The result was a fractured church and a damaged witness. The harm came not only from what was done, but from what was left undone. The same spirit of silence that plagued Eden now permeates pulpits, homes, and communities.

The fall fractured man's ability to lead. Shame ruled silently. Fear drove men to avoid leadership or twist it. Instead of serving under God, many dominated, manipulated, or withdrew.

Scripture is full of such failures, fathers who wounded their sons, kings who abused power, men who abandoned responsibility. The pattern has not changed. Today, countless men lead from insecurity, afraid of being exposed, desperate to prove themselves. And authority that is not rooted in grace promptly turns into a weapon instead of a gift.

The Second Adam

But praise God, the story does not end in Eden. Redemption comes through the Second Adam, Jesus Christ.

> "FOR AS BY THE ONE MAN'S DISOBEDIENCE THE MANY WERE MADE SINNERS, SO BY THE ONE MAN'S OBEDIENCE THE MANY WILL BE MADE RIGHTEOUS."
> ROMANS 5:19

Where Adam failed, Christ triumphed. He not only forgives, He restores manhood. He redeems leadership. In Him, men are freed from shame, strengthened by grace, and called to lead as God intended.

> "FOR THIS PURPOSE I WAS BORN AND FOR THIS PURPOSE I HAVE COME INTO THE WORLD, TO BEAR WITNESS TO THE TRUTH."
> JOHN 18:37

Where Adam blamed, Jesus bore the blame. Isaiah prophesies,

> "SURELY HE HAS BORNE OUR GRIEFS AND CARRIED OUR SORROWS...
> HE WAS PIERCED FOR OUR TRANSGRESSIONS."
> ISAIAH 53:4-5

Where Adam fled, Jesus stood firm. In Gethsemane, facing betrayal and death, Jesus prayed,

Grace That Restores

Still, the accuser whispers, *"You're not enough." "You're too broken." "You failed too many times."* But Scripture thunders back.

> "THERE IS THEREFORE NOW NO CONDEMNATION FOR THOSE WHO
> ARE IN CHRIST JESUS"
> ROMANS 8:1.

Grace silences guilt, not by pretending sin doesn't exist, but by declaring that Christ has paid it all. Titus 2:11-12 reminds us that God's grace both saves and trains us, to renounce ungodliness and live self-controlled, upright, and godly lives.

Biblical leadership does not begin with competence; it begins with surrender.

A former gang member, now a pastor, explained why he mentors at-risk youth: 'Grace gave me a second chance. Leadership is how I say thank you

The essence of redeemed leadership is not self-glory but response to grace.

Marks of a Redeemed Leader

Humility

Do I regularly confess my dependence on God in prayer?

Do I admit when I don't know something instead of pretending I do?

Do I celebrate others' successes without feeling threatened?

Initiative

Do I step forward to meet needs without waiting for someone else?

Do I take small, faithful steps when the outcome isn't guaranteed?

Do I model courage by acting when it costs me time, comfort, or reputation?

Repentance

Do I confess wrongs quickly instead of defending myself?

Do I restore relationships I have strained?

Do I regularly ask God to search my heart?

Teachability

Do I invite feedback, when it stings?

Do I carve out time for learning and growth?

Do I surround myself with mentors and accountability?

Faithfulness

Do I keep showing up when results are slow?

Do I resist shortcuts or compromises?

Do I finish what I start?

Faithfulness is the spine of biblical leadership. It is perseverance through trial, steadfastness against temptation, and service in obscurity. It isn't flashy but enduring, a long obedience in the same direction.

Faithfulness reflects God's own character, unchanging, reliable, steadfast.

Simple Steps

In 2023, one struggling church discovered the transformative power of initiative. Five men, weary of spiritual apathy, decided to gather for prayer. The beginning was small. No programs. No spotlight. Merely a burden and a decision to act.

What followed was remarkable. Their persistence in prayer sparked renewal. Within months, the congregation experienced a fresh awakening. What began with five men on their knees rippled outward into the life of an entire church.

This is the nature of initiative. Monumental change often begins with small, determined steps. It is the courage to assess the situation, identify the need, and move forward, when the path ahead feels uncertain.

God Uses the Broken

If you think you're disqualified, you're not. Scripture is full of broken men God used.

In 2022, Chuck Adair, a former inmate, planted a church in Texas and baptized 78 people in a single year. Since then, he has gone on to serve at Watermark Church in Dallas and mentor others through its Re:Generation ministry. This ministry is especially close to my heart, as I once had the privilege of leading it at my own church.

Chuck's past did not disqualify him. Instead, it became his pulpit. His story reflects the truth Paul proclaims

Though the enemy seeks to use Chuck's past against him, stirring up strife and discouragement, God uses those very experiences as a bridge to others who carry similar struggles. What the enemy intended for evil, the Creator has transformed and redeemed for His glory and for eternal good.

Chuck Adair's journey vividly illustrates the profound truth that our brokenness, when surrendered to God, becomes a tool for extraordinary ministry.

His life stands as a powerful testimony that no matter a person's past, God's grace is always sufficient. He redeems, He restores, and He intentionally employs surrendered lives for the advance of His Kingdom.

Why Men Shrink Back

If this is true, why do so many men hesitate to lead?

1. **Lack of role models**, raised without fathers or mentors, many men never witnessed authentic spiritual leadership.

2. **Fear of failure**, like Adam hiding in shame, men avoid leadership lest inadequacy be exposed.

3. **Expectation of perfection**, believing they must never stumble, they remain paralyzed.

But leadership is not perfection. It is faithfulness. It is showing up in weakness, trusting God's strength.

The Example of Christ

Jesus shows us true leadership:

- He sacrificed His life for His bride

- He restored the fallen

- He wept with the grieving

- He confronted injustice

- He welcomed the weary

This is headship: not dominance, but sacrificial love. Not control, but care. Not pride, but humility.

The Call Today

So, what does this mean for us? Start with small, faithful steps.

- Wake up early to pray.

- Repent to your family when you fail them.

- Open the Bible together at dinner.

- Lead a small group at church.

- Mentor a younger man.

Leadership is not a ladder to climb. It is a towel to carry.

True leadership is service. It is being available to talk, pray, and walk alongside others.

You were formed for this. Redeemed for this. Called for this. The garden may have been lost, but the mission remains. And in Christ, your leadership is not only possible but powerful.

Will you lead? Not by might, not by power, but by the Spirit of God.

Reflection

- Confess one area where you've led with pride, passivity, or fear, and surrender it to God.

- Choose one mark of a redeemed leader (humility, initiative, repentance, teachability, faithfulness) to practice this week.

- Take a small, concrete act of servant-leadership in your home, workplace, or church.

- Write down a past failure and then declare Christ's redeeming grace over it as your foundation for leadership.

Prayer

Father, thank You for redeeming my life and calling me to lead with purpose. I confess the places where I have been silent, fearful, or self-centered. Forgive me and restore my strength in You. Empower me with humility, courage, and sacrificial love. Let my life reflect Christ, bringing hope and blessing to those You've entrusted to me. In Jesus' name, Amen.

Walking in the Spirit

"But I say, walk by the Spirit, and you will not gratify the desires of the flesh." , Galatians 5:16

Every man knows that moment when conviction lands hard. Maybe it's a sermon that cuts through the noise, a wife's words that pierce excuses, or the quiet weight of Scripture pressing on the soul. Resolve flares. You whisper, *"Things must change."*

But then life presses in. The alarm blares. Deadlines pile up. Old temptations creep back. What felt unshakable fades like dew in the morning sun.

Why? Because conviction alone cannot carry transformation. Grit fails where grace must prevail. Resolutions forged in human strength crumble under pressure. True change is not the fruit of willpower but of daily dependence on the Spirit of God.

Willpower vs. Spirit-Power

Paul says it clearly when he says walk by the Spirit. Notice, he doesn't say, try harder or make bigger promises. He says walk. That word pictures steady, faithful steps, a daily reliance on God's power, not our own.

- **Willpower dries up.** The Spirit renews strength every morning.

- **Willpower bends under temptation.** The Spirit equips us with armor to stand firm.

- **Willpower says, "I've got this."** The Spirit declares,

"APART FROM CHRIST, YOU CAN DO NOTHING"
JOHN 15:5

Conviction matters. But conviction alone will not hold. The modern man doesn't need another pump-up speech or self-help plan. He needs grace. He needs supernatural strength.

Jesus was clear: *"Apart from Me you can do nothing."* Not some things. Not small things. **Nothing**.

Who Is the Spirit?

For many men, the Holy Spirit remains a mystery. They know God the Father. They love Jesus the Son. But the Spirit? To them, He feels vague, an energy, a mood, or just a theological afterthought.

This confusion is not new. Too often, the church has failed to paint a clear picture of the Spirit's role. As a result, men approach Him with uncertainty, or worse, with neglect.

Scripture leaves no room for confusion. The Spirit is not a force or mood; He is God Himself:

- **Divine**: Peter rebuked Ananias for lying to the Holy Spirit.
- **Helper** (*Parakletos*): Advocate, comforter, counselor
- **Spirit of Truth**
- **Indweller**: Our very bodies are His temple
- **Empowerer**: He equips us for mission
- **Producer of fruit**: Christlike character

Without Him, we are powerless, like a chainsaw without fuel. With Him, everything changes.

In Marriage

When conflict comes, and it will, the flesh wants to lash out, withdraw, or fight to win. Walking in the Spirit means pausing long enough to let grace interrupt your instinct.

- Softening your tone when you want to sharpen it.
- Praying before answering instead of preparing a counterattack.
- Choosing reconciliation over scoring points.

In those small Spirit-led choices, trust is restored, love is strengthened, and the home becomes a place of peace.

A husband comes home exhausted. His flesh wants to retreat to the recliner. Instead, he senses the Spirit nudging him to serve he listens to his wife, helps with the dishes, responds gently. That's walking in the Spirit.

In Fatherhood

The flesh parents from impatience or exhaustion. The Spirit calls you to father with patience and presence.

When your child fails, the flesh reacts with shame. The Spirit leads you to discipline firmly but with love, aiming not only to correct behavior but to shepherd the heart.

Walking in the Spirit as a father means letting your kids see humility in action, confessing when you blow it, asking forgiveness, and showing them that dependence on God is not weakness, but strength.

A father discovers his teenage son has been lying. The flesh reaction would be to explode in anger or shame him into obedience. Walking in the Spirit means he takes a breath, prays privately for wisdom, and addresses the sin firmly yet redemptively. He disciplines with fairness, explains why honesty matters to God, and reaffirms his love. The goal is not only to correct behavior but to shepherd the heart toward Christ.

At Work

The flesh bends toward grumbling, cutting corners, or chasing recognition. The Spirit calls you to integrity, kindness, and peace even in stressful environments.

A Spirit-led man is the same on Monday as he is on Sunday. His coworkers begin to see faith not only as a belief system but as a way of life.

A man is offered an opportunity to take shortcuts on a project to save time and impress his boss. His flesh whispers that it will make him look good. The Spirit reminds him that integrity matters more than short-term gain. He does the work honestly, if it costs him recognition. Later, when a coworker takes credit for something he contributed to, he resists bitterness, prays for them, and trusts God to be his rewarder.

Walking in the Spirit means daily dependence.

Listening for His voice through Scripture and prayer, tuning your ear to God's whisper.

Obeying His nudges in real time, following His lead whether in a boardroom, at the dinner table, or when temptation knocks.

This is not about trying harder but about trusting deeper. One path leaves you empty. The other leads you into life.

This is not mystical fluff. This is real boots on the ground, trench warfare discipleship. When temptation strikes, the Spirit offers the way out. When you have no words to pray, the Spirit groans on your behalf. When the fog of life rolls in, the Spirit becomes your compass.

The Tug of War Within

The flesh is relentless. It does not rest. Its voice may sound appealing, even reasonable, but its end is always the same: self-gratification at the expense of holiness, and slavery at the expense of freedom.

The flesh pulls us one way; the Spirit pulls us another.

That tension in your soul is not a sign you're losing, it's proof you're alive. A dead man feels no fight. Only the man made alive in Christ will feel this war within, because the Spirit in him refuses to let the flesh have the final word.

Dead men feel no tug-of-war; they are prone to collapse and are dragged without resistance. But a man indwelt by the Spirit feels the rope dig into his hands, senses the strain of the fight, and knows the Spirit is at work within him.

The battle is real, but so is the Helper. You don't fight alone. The Spirit is not simply pulling beside you; He is empowering you, bracing your feet, and assuring you that victory belongs to Christ.

The Interrupted Commute

Daniel was a young accountant who dreaded Monday mornings. One week, he was running late, traffic was heavy, and his mind was already racing through deadlines and meetings. As he sat at a red light, he noticed an older man on the sidewalk struggling with a flat tire. His first instinct was to look away. "I don't have time for this," he thought, gripping the steering wheel tighter.

But in that pause, he felt a nudge in his heart. Not a booming voice, but a quiet conviction: *Stop and help him.* Daniel sighed, pulled over, and offered a hand. The man's face lit up with relief. Within fifteen minutes, the tire was changed, and they were back on their way. As Daniel drove off, surprisingly, he felt lighter. His stress about the day seemed smaller, his heart felt fuller.

Later, as he reflected on the moment, Daniel realized something important. That nudge to stop was not his natural impulse. His flesh wanted convenience. The Spirit led him toward compassion. That small decision became a reminder that walking in the Spirit often looks like choosing love in the ordinary interruptions of life.

For Daniel, walking in the Spirit that morning meant surrendering his schedule, serving a stranger, and finding joy on a day that had started in frustration.

The Danger of Drift

In 2023, a high-profile pastor resigned in disgrace. His sin wasn't theft or heresy. It was an emotional affair that devastated trust and sent shockwaves through his congregation. The headlines captured the scandal, but the collapse didn't start in a hotel room. It started long before.

It began in skipped devotions. In shallow accountability. In neglected prayer. In the quiet erosion of intimacy with Christ. Sin scarcely kicks down the door. More often, it seeps in stealthily, through busyness, pride, and unchecked weariness.

Accountability, once sharp and honest, grew shallow. The brothers who once had full access to his heart were now filtered through assistants and polished PR. Too busy to meet. Too important to be questioned. Too exhausted to confess.

The drift toward compromise wasn't sudden. It was a thousand small surrenders. He didn't fall in a moment. He drifted, gradually but constantly, carried by a current he thought he could control.

"A LITTLE SLEEP, A LITTLE SLUMBER, A LITTLE FOLDING OF THE HANDS TO REST, AND POVERTY WILL COME UPON YOU LIKE A ROBBER, AND WANT LIKE AN ARMED MAN."
PROVERBS 24:33-34

Substitute spiritual discipline for sleep and you have a blueprint for moral failure. A little skipped prayer. A little isolation. A little pride. Suddenly, poverty of the soul takes root.

The truth is that drift is not stillness. Drift is movement, but always in the wrong direction. It doesn't leave you where you were; it pulls you where you never intended to go. David thought he was simply staying home, taking a season of rest. He was already moving, away from his calling, away from his brothers, and ultimately, away from his God.

Guardrails of Grace

To resist drift, men must build safeguards:

- Radical vigilance: staying alert to the subtle slide of compromise.
- Regular confession: keeping short accounts with God.
- Accountability: inviting brothers to be watchmen over our souls.
- Daily devotion: prayer, Scripture, worship, stillness before God.

Faithfulness requires both cultivation and protection.

Healing in the Light

Victory begins with confession. It deepens through accountability. And it grows as we feed daily on the Word and lean on the Spirit in moments of weakness. What God did for Shane, He can do for you. The chains may feel unbreakable, but the Spirit is stronger.

So, ask yourself: Where am I fighting alone? Where have I chosen silence instead of confession, or willpower instead of Spirit-dependence? Bring that struggle into the light. Invite the Spirit to take control. Freedom is not a distant dream; it is the promise of life in Christ.

We must never retreat into the shadows of secrecy, shame, or self-pity. Those places only deepen barrenness and magnify temptation. The Holy Spirit is faithful, always ready to convict, to comfort, and to restore. But His work can be stifled if we harden our hearts.

We quench Him when pride keeps us from confessing, when distractions drown out His voice, when self-reliance replaces dependence. The Spirit whispers, but the noise of the world shouts. The choice is ours: will we humble ourselves, listen, and yield?

Openness and responsiveness are the gateway to transformation. When we drop the masks and bow low, we find that the Spirit does what only He can, renew, empower, and make us whole.

And when, not if, you fall? The Spirit doesn't walk away. He draws near.

"WRETCHED MAN THAT I AM! WHO WILL DELIVER ME?" THE ANSWER COMES IMMEDIATELY: "THANKS BE TO GOD THROUGH JESUS CHRIST OUR LORD!".
ROMANS 7:24

A Spirit-filled man doesn't glow in the dark. He hugs his kids. He makes coffee. He serves his wife. He prays when he's tired. He forgives when it's costly. He shows up when no one's watching.

You were not designed to grit your way through life. You were made to walk, step by step, day by day, in the power of the Spirit. Your family is watching. Your church is waiting. The world is desperate. Will you rise?

The Spirit is willing. Are you?

Reflection

- Identify where you have been relying on willpower instead of the Spirit's power.

- Confess the fruit of the flesh that still wars within you and ask the Spirit to replace it with His fruit.

- Commit to one daily habit this week that keeps you in step with the Spirit (prayer, Scripture, silence before God).

- Invite a trusted brother to walk with you in accountability and prayer.

Prayer

Holy Spirit, I surrender my strength and my pride. I confess my weakness and my wandering. Lead me. Fill me. Empower me. Let Your fruit grow in me, love, joy, peace, patience, kindness, goodness, faithfulness, gentleness, and self-control. Align my mind, words, and habits with Christ, so my life bears witness to Your power. In Jesus' name, Amen.

Love as Christ Loved

"Husbands, love your wives, as Christ loved the church and gave himself up for her..." Ephesians 5:25

Paul's command in Ephesians is radical. It will not fit neatly into cultural expectations. It confronts pride. It challenges selfishness. It unsettles comfort.

Notice what Paul does *not* say. He does not write, *"Love your wife when she respects you."* He does not add, *"Lead her only when she agrees with you."* Every qualifier vanishes under the weight of this command. The standard is Christ Himself, who laid down His life for His bride.

True leadership is not about privilege or control. It is about sacrifice. It means bleeding before blaming. Serving before demanding. Protecting before presuming. To lead like Jesus is to die to self so that your wife may flourish.

And for men who are not married, the call still echoes.

The same sacrificial love that defines a husband's role also shapes how you honor women as sisters in Christ. It governs how you treat them, with dignity, purity, and respect. It fuels how you serve faithfully in your church. It directs how you mentor the next generation and invest in friendships that last.

Whether single, divorced, or widowed, the assignment does not change. The call is the same: to embody Christ's self-giving love in whatever season or station God has placed you.

This is not about the fleeting rush of infatuation or the comforts of domestic romance. Paul's words are deeper.

For husbands, this is not theory, it is a daily, deliberate choice. It is the choice to prioritize your wife's well-being and spiritual flourishing above your own. It is the choice to be patient when you want to snap, to forgive when you would rather withdraw, and to serve when it costs time, ambition, or pride.

Some men carry wounds that make sacrificial love more complicated, and this reality must be acknowledged with honesty and compassion. Past experiences of rejection, betrayal, abuse, or abandonment can leave scars that make trust difficult, and vulnerability feel dangerous.

These wounds do not excuse neglecting the call to love, but they do help explain why some men struggle to give of themselves fully. Recognizing this tension allows us to extend grace while also encouraging healing, reminding men that Christ meets them in their brokenness and equips them to love in ways they could not in their own strength.

Love, as defined by Scripture, is not based on feelings but on sacrifice. John puts it plainly:

"THIS IS HOW WE KNOW WHAT LOVE IS: JESUS CHRIST LAID DOWN HIS
LIFE FOR US"
1 JOHN 3:16.

This love is gritty, raw, and relentless. Not something that's earned, it is initiated. It moves first. It absorbs the hit. It does not flinch. For husbands, it means loving your wife when she is weary, when she is difficult, when she is silent, and when she is radiant. It is the steady, cruciform love of Christ expressed in daily choices.

Divorced or widowed men are likewise called to embody this love. Your witness shines as you mentor, protect, and carry burdens within God's family.

Every man is called to this kind of love because every man is called to reflect Christ. Whether in marriage, singleness, fatherhood, or brotherhood, the measure is the same: lay down your life so others may flourish.

Look at what Jesus did. He left glory for grit. He stepped into humanity's mess. He bore rejection, betrayal, mockery, torture, and death—not for a faithful bride, but for a wandering one.

That is the standard. You want to know how to lead? Start with a cross. Not a throne. Not a spotlight. A cross. However, if we want to recover a biblical vision of manhood, we must kill a few lies.

Lie #1: Headship is Dictatorship

If your version of headship looks like barking orders while your wife walks on eggshells, you're not a leader, you're a tyrant. That is not biblical manhood; it is sin. True headship looks like Christ. It means you take the first blow, you lay your life down, you walk into the fire, not away from it. Paul writes:

"THE HUSBAND IS THE HEAD OF THE WIFE EVEN AS CHRIST IS THE HEAD OF THE CHURCH, HIS BODY, AND IS HIMSELF ITS SAVIOR" EPHESIANS 5:23.

Lie #2: Headship is Passivity

As dangerous as domination is abdication. Some men hide behind silence, leaving their wives to carry the spiritual and emotional weight of the family. But passivity is not humility, it's neglect. God did not call Adam to watch the serpent speak; He called him to guard and lead. A godly man refuses to drift. He steps up when it's costly, because love takes initiative.

Lie #3: Headship is Perfection

Some men avoid leading because they feel disqualified by their flaws. But leadership in marriage is not about flawless performance, it's about faithful dependence. Christlike headship is not sinless but surrendered. When you stumble, you repent first. When you fail, you confess quickly. Your family doesn't need a perfect man. They need a humble one who keeps pointing them to a perfect Savior.

And these lies don't just creep into marriage. Dictatorship shows up at work or in friendships when you control instead of serving. Passivity surfaces when you coast spiritually and leave others to carry the weight. Perfectionism whispers you can't lead until you "have it all together." Don't believe it.

The call is the same in every season: lead through service, step forward instead of shrinking back, and walk humbly in dependence on Christ.

What Headship Really Is

Christ didn't use His position to serve Himself. He leveraged His authority to rescue and restore His bride. That's biblical headship: not self-centered authority, but sacrificial responsibility.

Jesus served. He wept at graves. He carried a cross not His own. He prayed for those who betrayed Him. That's your model. As one Christian counselor put it, *"Most men think headship means they get to make the final call. No. It means they get to take the first hit."*

Headship means being the first to repent, the first to pray, the first to apologize, the first to ask, *"How's your heart?"* You don't wait for your wife to earn tenderness; you offer it preemptively, just as Christ loved us while we were still sinners.

And yes, it will cost you. It will cost your pride when she calls you out. Your energy when she needs you after a long day. Your preferences, hobbies, and comfort. But if you're not ready to bleed for your bride, you're not ready to lead your bride.

Biblical headship is not a throne of privilege; it is a cross of sacrifice. Christ didn't lead His bride with domination but with crucifixion. The husband doesn't ask, *"What do I get out of this?"* but *"What can I give for her good and God's glory?"*

Practical Expressions of Leadership

So, what does this look like day to day?

- **Spiritually:** You are the pastor of your family. That doesn't mean formal sermons at the dinner table, but it does mean setting the tone. Open Scripture together, even just a few verses. Pray for and with your wife and children. Let them see your dependence on God. In doing so, you guide not as a lecturer but as a fellow traveler pointing to Christ.

- **Emotionally:** Pursue her heart. Ask about her dreams and fears. Notice her rhythms and cues. Don't settle for distracted nods while scrolling your phone, look her in the eye and listen. To understand is to study her like the most intricate book God ever wrote.

- **Physically and Tangibly:** Love is embodied in touch, tone, and time. A gentle embrace at the end of a hard day. A soft tone when irritation tempts you. Paul warns:

"HUSBANDS, LOVE YOUR WIVES AND DO NOT BE HARSH WITH THEM"
COLOSSIANS 3:19

Harshness can be silence, clipped answers, or an impatient sigh. But tenderness, holding her hand in prayer, walking beside her, speaking kindly, builds safety and intimacy.

Gentleness is not weakness; it is strength under control. Studies confirm what Scripture has long declared: emotional safety is the strongest predictor of marital satisfaction. And emotional safety is built not in grand gestures, but in daily choices, soft tone, listening ear, gentle touch.

The Call to Pursue

Pursuit doesn't end with the wedding vows. Christ never stopped pursuing His bride. Neither should you. Plan dates, surprise her with small acts of kindness, learn her love language, keep asking questions. Love that stops learning soon grows stale.

And when you fail, and you will… repent quickly. Your wife doesn't need perfection; she needs repentance. A man who stumbles but keeps pointing to Christ leads far better than one who hides behind pride.

Biblical headship is covenantal, not convenient. It doesn't tap out when feelings fade. It leans in. It endures. It fights for unity, not victory. It dies daily.

The Hospital Chair

John and Maria had been married for over twenty years when Maria was diagnosed with a serious illness. For months, her treatment left her weak and weary. John rearranged his work schedule, learned how to cook her favorite meals, and sat by her hospital bed night after night. Nurses often found him asleep in a chair, holding her hand, refusing to leave when visiting hours ended.

One evening, a nurse quietly asked him, "Why do you stay here every night? You could rest at home." John smiled and whispered, "Because she stayed with me through all my storms. I made a vow before God to love her in sickness and in health. This is what that vow looks like."

Love is not a feeling that fades with circumstances. It is a decision to give, to serve, and to sacrifice.

John's love did not make the illness disappear, but it gave Maria strength and dignity in the middle of suffering. It mirrored the kind of love Christ shows His church: steadfast, selfless, and unwavering.

True biblical manhood is not about demanding respect. It is about laying down our lives for those entrusted to us. Just as Christ's love was proven on the cross, a husband's love is proven in the quiet, costly acts of service that say, "Your good matters more than my comfort."

Where to Begin

Start with repentance. If you've led with pride, been passive, or acted harshly, confess it. Grace is not an excuse to stay the same; it's power to start again.

Pray daily, for her soul, her dreams, her fears, her burdens, and let her hear you do it. Lead consistently, not with bravado but with faithfulness.

The world does not need more arrogant men. It needs more crucified men, men who lead with a limp, love with a cross, and live with an open Bible.

That is your calling. Now go and live it.

Reflection

- Identify where your love has been self-serving rather than sacrificial.

- Confess areas where apathy has replaced active pursuit of your wife's heart.

- Commit to one practical way this week to lead your wife spiritually with consistency.

- Choose one daily habit that will help you reflect Christ's love more fully.

Prayer

Jesus, thank You for loving me with a sacrificial love I did not deserve. Teach me to love my wife with that same humility and faithfulness. Shape my words to be gentle, my actions to be patient, and my leadership to be anchored in Your Word. Let my marriage reflect Your gospel and bring You glory. In Your name, Amen.

Christlike Communication

"Let every person be quick to hear, slow to speak, slow to anger."
James 1:19

Many marriages do not collapse in an explosion of betrayal. They crumble slowly, almost imperceptibly.

It happens through the erosion of communication. Words become transactional. Conversations stay shallow. Assumptions silently replace understanding.

Without consistent connection, the emotional bond begins to wither. A marriage deprived of meaningful communication is like a house with cracks in its foundation. It may still be standing, but it grows fragile and vulnerable to collapse.

When Words Matter

Cliff and Helen had been married for seven years when the silence between them began to feel louder than their words. It started small: Cliff came home late from work, too tired to share about his day, while Helen longed for conversation and connection.

She dropped subtle hints, sighs at the dinner table, questions asked halfheartedly, but he missed them. When she finally voiced her frustration, Cliff heard only criticism. He retreated further; she pressed harder. Their exchanges became sharp and defensive.

One night, after a bitter argument that ended with Helen in tears and Cliff slamming the bedroom door, both lay awake in separate rooms, wondering how they had drifted so far. They still loved each other, but the current of misunderstanding kept pulling them apart.

The turning point came months later in a counselor's office. There, Cliff heard for the first time not just what Helen was saying, but the heart beneath it: she felt invisible. And Helen began to realize that Cliff's long hours were not avoidance, but fear. He feared failing as a provider, and he feared letting her down.

There was not an instant fix. Learning to communicate meant practicing uncomfortable habits: repeating back what they heard before responding, asking questions instead of assuming motives, and setting aside time each week for honest, distraction-free conversations. Cliff had to learn to look Helen in the eyes and listen without rushing to solve. Helen had to learn to voice her needs without blame.

Over time, their words became bridges instead of weapons. Small victories such as a calm talk after a disagreement or a late-night laugh over miscommunication reminded them that growth was possible. Where silence once bred resentment, conversation began to sow intimacy.

Their story became one of redemption, not because conflict disappeared, but because they learned how to speak, listen, and forgive. The failure of their communication became the soil where deeper understanding could finally grow.

Why Words Matter

Biblical communication goes beyond exchanging information. It cultivates intimacy, pursues unity, and honors the image of God in your spouse.

"A WORD FITLY SPOKEN IS LIKE APPLES OF GOLD IN A SETTING OF SILVER."

PROVERBS 25:11

Words, when chosen with grace, can heal wounds, restore hope, and draw two hearts closer.

In marriage, words are never neutral. They either build or break, nourish or neglect, bless or bruise.

Enemies of Intimacy

To guard your marriage, you must recognize the subtle habits that erode connection:

Sarcasm – words that cut instead of heal.

Stonewalling – withdrawing in silence, which communicates rejection.

Distraction – giving your phone, work, or hobbies more attention than your spouse.

Assumptions – deciding you already "know" what they think.

Harshness – sharp tones or impatient sighs that wound more than words.

Left unchecked, these habits create an atmosphere where love withers and suspicion grows.

Spirit-Filled Communication

By contrast, Spirit-filled habits breathe life into a marriage:

Active Listening – hearing not only words but the heart behind them.

Gentle Speech – tones that build trust, even in conflict.

Encouragement – affirming your spouse's value.

Honest Confession – admitting wrongs and seeking forgiveness.

Scripture-Shaped Words – letting God's Word guide your speech.

Practiced habitually, these turn ordinary conversations into sacred moments of connection.

A Blueprint for Marriage

"Let every person be quick to hear, slow to speak, slow to anger."

This triad is not casual advice but Spirit-inspired wisdom.

Quick to Hear – Listening with humility, seeking to understand before responding. To listen well is to love well.

Slow to Speak – Exercising restraint. Waiting until words can be shaped by grace, not impulse.

Slow to Anger – Responding with gentleness rather than irritation. A husband who leads with calm models the heart of Christ.

Picture this scenario. Your wife sighs, "You're never present when you get home." The flesh wants to snap back: *"Do you know how hard I work?"*

James 1:19 redirects: pause, listen, soften your tone, and ask, "Help me understand what you need from me." What could have spiraled into a fight becomes a chance for connection.

The Power of Words

Words shape the climate of a marriage.

Mark once brushed off sarcasm as humor. But over time, Sarah felt dismissed. Finally, she admitted, "I don't feel safe talking to you anymore." Convicted, Mark repented. He began choosing words that built her up. Gradually, their home shifted from sarcasm to affirmation.

Careless words cut like swords. Wise words bring healing.

Christlike Communication in Action

Jesus Himself modeled this pattern. On the road to Emmaus, He listened first, then spoke truth. He leaned in with patience before proclamation.

A modern story illustrates the same:

Not long ago, a video circulated that captured a moment between a husband and wife during one of her anxiety attacks. In the clip, you can see her breathing quicken and her hands tremble as panic overtakes her. Many in that situation might have minimized her struggle, saying things like, *"Calm down, you're fine"* or *"Just breathe."* But this husband did something different.

He gently took her hand, steadied her trembling, and began to pray Scripture over her. His voice was calm, steady, and full of compassion. He whispered words from the Psalms:

"THE LORD IS MY SHEPHERD; I SHALL NOT WANT... HE RESTORES MY SOUL."
PSALM 23

He spoke Isaiah's promise:

"YOU KEEP HIM IN PERFECT PEACE WHOSE MIND IS STAYED ON YOU"
ISAIAH 26:3

He reminded her that she was safe, loved, and held not only by him but by the God who never leaves or forsakes His children.

The effect was remarkable. Slowly, her breathing steadied, her tears began to slow, and she leaned into his embrace as his prayers washed over her. The video went viral, shared by thousands who were struck by the tenderness of the moment. One comment summed it up best: *"I've never seen a man pray with his wife like that. That's real love."*

What made the video so moving wasn't just that he prayed , it was how he prayed. His words were not lectures, not quick fixes, not empty reassurances. They were life-giving words, rooted in the promises of God. He didn't try to control her feelings or solve the problem in his own strength. He chose instead to lift her to the One who could calm the storm inside her heart.

That is Christlike communication, presence, patience, prayer.

By contrast, silence and neglect wound deeply. A friend once said, *"My dad never yelled. He just shut down. For years, I thought I wasn't worth engaging."* Not all wounds are loud. Sometimes silence cuts deepest.

The Dinner Table

Ethan had just come home from a long day at work. He was tired, frustrated, and ready to relax. As soon as he sat down, his wife mentioned a bill that had gone unpaid. Irritation flared. His voice rose sharply: "Why didn't you handle it earlier?" The words landed like stones. Silence filled the room, and his wife's eyes dropped to her plate.

Conviction came almost instantly. Ethan knew his tone had cut deeper than the issue itself. He excused himself, went into the bedroom, and prayed. *"Lord, set a guard over my mouth. Teach me to speak life, not death"*.

When he returned, he sat back down and gently said, "I'm sorry. I spoke harshly, and that wasn't fair to you. The bill matters, but you matter more." His wife's eyes softened, and the wall between them began to crumble.

Christlike communication is not about never failing. It is about being quick to listen, slow to speak, and willing to repair when words wound. Ethan learned that his words could either tear down or build up. When surrendered to Christ, they could become instruments of grace:

That night, a simple apology and a humble change of tone turned conflict into connection. His home shifted from tension to peace because he chose to speak as Christ would.

Understanding Your Wife

"Live with your wives in an understanding way... so that your prayers may not be hindered."

This is more than practical wisdom, it is a spiritual mandate. To disregard your wife's heart is to jeopardize fellowship with God.

Being a student of your wife means asking:

- What causes her stress?
- What brings her joy?
- How does she feel loved and connected?
- What fears or past wounds shape her responses?

Understanding requires intentional listening, empathy, and consistency. Many wives don't say, "*I feel unloved.*" They say, "*I feel unseen.*" To truly see your wife is to reflect Christ's own love for His Church.

Barriers to Healthy Communication

- **Pride** – makes us defensive and dismissive.
- **Fear** – of failure or rejection, silences us.
- **Distraction** – crowded schedules and screens drown out attention.

Practical tools help:

- Weekly check-ins.

- Reflective listening (repeat back what you heard).
- Using "I" statements instead of accusations.
- Pausing and praying before answering.
- Daily prayer together.
- These small habits create safety and rebuild connections.

Rebuilding Trust

Even the most faithful couples face seasons of drought. Love does not disappear, but misunderstandings pile up like stones until they form a wall. Harsh words echo louder than kind ones, and silence stretches longer than it should. In those moments, the temptation is to pull back, to withhold affection, or to seek revenge in subtle ways. Yet Scripture calls us to something higher:

"IF POSSIBLE, SO FAR AS IT DEPENDS ON YOU, LIVE PEACEABLY WITH ALL."
ROMANS 12:18

Peace is not passive. It is the active pursuit of reconciliation.

Closing Exhortation

Communication is not optional. It is the bloodstream of your marriage.

- You do not need a silver tongue; you need a humble heart.
- You do not need to be a poet; you need to be present.

Invite the Holy Spirit into your tone, your words, and even your silence.

When your words carry grace, your marriage becomes a sanctuary of healing and a testimony of the gospel.

That is the essence of Christlike communication. Words that could have wounded were turned into words that healed. Where silence could have left a scar, a father's gentle reply planted courage and hope.

> "A WORD FITLY SPOKEN IS LIKE APPLES OF GOLD IN SETTINGS OF
> SILVER."
> PROVERBS 25:11

Reflection

- Identify one recent moment where you listened well and one where you failed to genuinely hear your wife.

- Evaluate the tone you use when frustrated and note how it impacts her sense of safety.

- Confess ways you've neglected emotional connection through avoidance, sarcasm, or distraction.

- Commit to one concrete step this week, whether it's asking deeper questions, setting aside device-free time, or affirming her feelings, strengthening your communication.

Prayer

Father, thank You for Your Word that guides my heart and my speech. Teach me to listen with patience, to speak with gentleness, and to love with sacrifice. Forgive me for careless words and inattentive ears. Fill me with Your Spirit so that my words bring life and my presence reflects Christ. In Jesus' name, Amen.

Conflict, Forgiveness, Grace

"Be kind to one another, tenderhearted, forgiving one another, as God in Christ forgave you." Ephesians 4:32

Ethan and Claire had been married for twelve years. They loved each other passionately, but recently, their marriage felt like a worn rope, frayed, pulled tight, and one sharp tug away from snapping. The stress of his long work hours and her full-time job mixed with the exhaustion of raising two young kids had created a constant undercurrent of tension.

Then on a Tuesday night the argument erupted.

Dinner had gone cold while Ethan sat in the driveway finishing a phone call from work. Claire, already frazzled from homework battles and spilled milk, met him at the door with a sharp, *"Do you even care about this family anymore?"*

The words stung. Instead of listening, Ethan fired back. His voice rose. Hers rose higher.

Old wounds from months past resurfaced like ghosts, times she felt unseen, moments he felt unappreciated. Then, in a flash of anger, Ethan turned toward the sink and slammed a plate onto the counter. It slipped from his hand and shattered on the floor.

The sound was like a gunshot in the kitchen.

The kids went silent. Claire's eyes filled with tears. Ethan froze, chest heaving, staring at the shards at his feet. In that moment, the Spirit's conviction hit him hard. This was not the man, or the husband, God had called him to be.

Without another word, he walked out to the porch and sat in the dark. Minutes passed before Claire stepped outside. She stood in the doorway, arms crossed, still hurt but willing to listen.

Ethan did not make excuses. He did not shift the blame.

"I'm sorry," he spoke quietly. "Not just for tonight, for the way I've been letting my frustration speak louder than my love. You deserve better. I've been wrong."

Claire hesitated, then sat down beside him. "I haven't been listening to you either," she admitted. "I've been assuming the worst instead of believing the best."

They sat together, shoulders touching, letting the night air cool their anger. No magic words fixed everything in that moment, but something shifted. Forgiveness began to replace resentment. Grace started to fill the cracks. They prayed right there on the porch, asking God to help them guard their words, to listen before speaking, and to love each other as Christ loved them.

Weeks later, when Ethan walked in late again, Claire greeted him with a hug instead of an accusation. And when she snapped at him in frustration one evening, he took her hand instead of raising his voice. The dishes stayed intact, but more significantly, so did their marriage.

Conflict in marriage is not the exception; it is the norm. Not reserved for the spiritually immature, the incompatible, or the unequally yoked. It is common ground, a shared battlefield, and often a crucible of sanctification. Even the most devoted Christian couples, those who attend church weekly, lead Bible studies, and pray before every meal, will still face tension, misunderstanding, and disagreement.

Conflict Is Normal

Conflict is not proof of a broken marriage. It is proof that two sinners are sharing life in close quarters.

Jesus never sugarcoated reality. He gave both a sober warning and a hopeful promise:

> *"IN THIS WORLD YOU WILL HAVE TROUBLE. BUT TAKE HEART; I HAVE OVERCOME THE WORLD."*
> *JOHN 16:33*

Trouble comes in many forms: disagreements about money, sexual intimacy, parenting styles, in-laws, time management, or unmet expectations. Conflict is part of life in a fallen world. The real issue is not whether conflict appears, but how we choose to respond when it does.

Adam and Eve's transgression, the very first sin committed, unleashed far more than just physical death into the world. It introduced a profound and pervasive state of division. This schism manifested on multiple levels: a severed relationship with God, a fractured connection between humanity, and even an internal disunion within individuals themselves.

Think of conflict like fire. In the hands of the careless, it burns, scars, and destroys. In the hands of the wise, it warms, purifies, and forges something stronger. The difference lies not in the fire itself, but in how it is handled. In the same way, the presence of conflict in your marriage is inevitable, but whether it becomes a destructive blaze or a refining flame depends on how you respond.

Consider David and Saul. The friction between them revealed Saul's insecurity, jealousy, and bitterness. At the same time, it revealed David's humility, patience, and trust in the Lord's timing.

What Conflict Reveals

Conflict does not just create character; it exposes it. Saul's jealousy revealed insecurity. David's restraint revealed trust in God.

In marriage, a fight about finances or parenting rarely stays on the surface. It reveals pride, fear, or selfishness within. Every conflict becomes a fork in the road, toward hardness of heart and bitterness, or toward holiness and deeper intimacy.

Conflict always brings a decision. One road leads to hardness. Bitterness grows. Distance widens. Another road leads to holiness. Forgiveness flows. Humility draws hearts close again. The struggle that might destroy becomes, with God's help, the very thing that unites.

And here's the paradox: the closer you grow to Christ, the more you will feel this tension. Why? Because the Spirit is at war with the flesh.

In moments of conflict, you're not just clashing with your spouse's flaws, you're clashing with your own. Marriage simply provides the mirror, and conflict makes sure you can't look away.

Let's be honest: sometimes conflict is unavoidable. You're tired, she's hormonal, the baby just threw up on the couch, and the credit card bill just hit. It's a perfect storm of circumstances that can easily ignite a disagreement.

In those moments, when emotions are high and patience is thin, you are presented with a crucial choice: you can escalate the situation, pouring fuel on the fire, or you can choose to edify, building up your spouse even amid tension.

Responding in the Spirit

The Apostle Paul understood this when he urged believers,

"DO NOT LET ANY UNWHOLESOME TALK COME OUT OF YOUR MOUTHS,
BUT ONLY WHAT IS HELPFUL FOR BUILDING OTHERS UP."
EPHESIANS 4:29

Notice, he doesn't exempt the heat of the moment. He doesn't say, "unless you're exhausted, unless she snapped first, unless the kids are driving you crazy." The command stands firm even in chaos.

That's where the Spirit's power becomes more than a doctrine, it becomes your lifeline. Left to your flesh, you'll lash out, withdraw, or fight to win the argument.

But walking in the Spirit means pausing long enough to let grace interrupt your instinct. It may look like you take a deep breath before you answer. It may sound like a soft tone when you'd rather raise your voice. It may simply be a whispered prayer in the middle of the mess.

These Spirit-led choices may seem small, but they shift the entire trajectory, from destruction to growth, from pride to humility, from division to deeper unity.

Because here's the truth: conflict doesn't have to be a wedge. If stewarded with humility, it can be a workshop. A place where patience is practiced, forgiveness is forged, and intimacy is deepened.

You can choose to attack, seeking to wound with your words, or you can choose to address the issue with grace and understanding. In the end, you can aim to win the argument, at the cost of your relationship, or you can aim to win your spouse's heart, preserving the intimacy and trust that is so vital to a healthy marriage.

Indeed, conflict, when stewarded well, can paradoxically be one of the most refining tools in a marriage. It forces growth, pushing both individuals beyond their comfort zones. It calls out idols, revealing what we prioritize above God and our spouse. It strips away the superficial and exposes the core values of our relationship.

The Apostle James offers a battle plan: *"Be quick to hear, slow to speak, slow to anger."*

This triad turns conflict from a battlefield into a classroom. The tension no longer becomes about *winning* but about *learning*, about seeing your spouse's heart, naming your own blind spots, and allowing the Spirit to shape both of you into Christ's likeness.

If you rush to be heard, prioritizing your own voice and perspective, you are not leading like Christ. You are leading like a fool. Pride and self-interest become your compass, and the result is damage to the very relationship you are called to cherish and protect.

Be Reconciled

Trey and Diane's marriage had reached a breaking point. Years of unspoken disappointment and sharp words had built a wall between them. One night after another heated argument, Diane packed a bag and drove to her sister's house. Trey sat alone in the quiet kitchen, staring at the half-empty coffee cups on the table. For the first time, he admitted to himself that he might lose her.

The next morning, Trey did something he had not done in years. He got on his knees and prayed, not for Diane to change, but for God to change him. Tears came as he confessed his pride, his harshness, and his failure to truly love her. Later that day, he drove to her sister's home. With no speech prepared, he simply looked at Diane and said, "I was wrong. I have hurt you. Please forgive me."

Diane had braced herself for excuses or defensiveness, but what she heard instead broke her. The anger that had kept her heart locked away began to melt. She wept, and for the first time in months, they embraced without words. This wasn't the end of their struggles, but it was the beginning of something new.

From that moment forward, Trey and Diane committed to walking the road of reconciliation. They sought counseling, they prayed together each night, and they set aside time every week just to talk. Slowly, trust returned. Laughter found its way back into their home. What had seemed impossible became a testimony of grace.

Their marriage was not saved by clever arguments or sheer willpower, but by humility, confession, and forgiveness. In giving up their pride, they found each other again. What once looked like ruins became a story of redemption.

Five Steps for Christlike Conflict

- Self-Examination - Start by asking: *"Have I been absent, harsh, selfish?"*.

- Confession Before Confrontation - Begin with your own faults. *"I've been wrong."*.

- Speak Life - Soft answers turn away wrath. Replace "You never" with "I feel."

- Forgive Completely - Forgive as Christ forgave, Let go of resentment and leverage.

- Pursue Reconciliation, Not Resolution - Don't just end arguments, restore intimacy.

So how do you deal with conflict God's way? Start with humility. Pride fuels conflict; humility diffuses it. reminds us,

"DO NOTHING FROM SELFISH AMBITION OR CONCEIT, BUT IN HUMILITY COUNT OTHERS MORE SIGNIFICANT THAN YOURSELVES."
PHILIPPIANS 2:3

Apologize first. Own your part. Be the first to say, *"I was wrong. Will you forgive me?"*

Then, practice active listening. That means no eye-rolling, no interrupting, and no rehearsing your rebuttal while she's talking. Repeat what she said to make sure you understand. Ask questions. Validate her emotions if you don't agree with her interpretation. Connection matters more than being correct.

Also, be solution-oriented, not score-keeping. The goal is not to count wins and losses. The goal is unity. Keep short accounts. Don't let a week pass without resolving the issue. Bitterness is a slow, silent killer.

And above all, invite God into the fight. Pray before, during, and after conflict. Ask the Holy Spirit to reveal your blind spots. Ask God for the grace to speak truth in love. When Christ is at the center of your marriage, even the hardest conflicts become opportunities for grace.

Jason and Emily

Jason and Emily's marriage looked calm from the outside. Friends would have called them "steady," but the truth was more complicated. When conflict arose, Jason's default was to disappear, not physically, but emotionally. If Emily confronted him about feeling overlooked, he'd give short answers, retreat to the garage, or bury himself in weekend fishing trips. He told himself he was "avoiding a fight," but Emily felt like she was married to a roommate.

Then came the breaking point. Emily brought up a financial decision he'd made without telling her. This time, Jason didn't retreat, he erupted. He raised his voice, threw out accusations, and ended the conversation with a slammed door. The silence that followed felt heavier than the argument itself.

Then during a men's Bible study Jason realized both of his responses, withdrawal and domination, were forms of self-protection, not love. Christ never withdrew from hard conversations, and He never ruled through fear. Instead, He engaged with truth and grace, when it cost Him comfort.

Convicted, Jason went home that night and told Emily, "I've been wrong in the way I handle our disagreements. I've either left you alone in the silence or crushed you with my words. I want to start handling conflict the way Christ would, with honesty, humility, and love." It didn't erase the hurt overnight, but it opened the door for a new way forward.

In all His interactions, Jesus was reliably firm in His principles, yet never furious in His delivery. He was bold in His pronouncements of truth but never belittling in His interactions with individuals. He embodied a paradox: He was the safest person in any room, offering unconditional acceptance and love, while simultaneously being the most truthful, unwilling to compromise on righteousness. This remarkable balance of grace and truth sets the ultimate standard for how we are called to interact with a broken world and with one another.

James slices through the surface of most marital disputes:

"WHAT CAUSES QUARRELS AND WHAT CAUSES FIGHTS AMONG YOU? IS IT NOT THIS, THAT YOUR PASSIONS ARE AT WAR WITHIN YOU?"
JAMES 4:1-2

Most arguments are not about what they seem. The toothpaste cap, the thermostat, or the in-law visit is not the root. The real issue is usually pride, fear, or selfishness. Pride boasts, "*I must be right.*" Fear proclaims, "*I can't be vulnerable.*" Selfishness whispers, "*My needs matter more than yours.*" Those are the enemies.

When we recognize that our own sinful desires fuel many of our conflicts, everything changes. The goal is not now to win the argument, but to defeat the sin within. We stop aiming our frustration at our spouse and start waging war in our own hearts. That's gospel-centered marriage. That's how we turn the battlefield into a vineyard.

It Is Everywhere

Recent headlines are sobering. In 2023 alone, multiple high-profile Christian leaders filed for divorce. The press releases declared things like *"irreconcilable differences"* or used words like *"amicable separation."* But behind the PR language were years of bitterness, emotional detachment, and spiritual drift. Conflict was not the villain. Neglect was. Pride and passivity left unchecked will choke a marriage to death.

Now, contrast that with the stories no one tweets. The couple that spent two years recovering from an affair, clinging to the Word and each other. The husband finally confessed his pornography addiction, wept in front of his wife, and started meeting with a pastor every week.

The wife who let go of years of bitterness, not because her husband earned it, but because Christ demanded it. These stories hardly ever trend. But in heaven, they are headline news.

A Christlike husband does not avoid hard conversations. He initiates them. He does not demand to be heard. He seeks to understand. He does not use silence as a weapon or anger as a hammer. He pursues peace with humility, patience, and purpose. He does not seek to win. He seeks to unite.

When to Seek Help

Some wounds cut deeper. Infidelity. Abuse. Abandonment. These do not heal overnight. But healing is still possible. Proverbs 11:14 says, "In an abundance of counselors there is safety." Don't white-knuckle your way through it. Get help. Biblical counseling is not a sign of failure. It's a sign of wisdom.

I once met a couple through counseling whose story still lingers with me. Their marriage, once vibrant, affectionate, and marked by joy, was bit by bit suffocated by the husband's decade-long addiction to pornography.

The turning point came in a single, agonizing moment of honesty. Unable to carry the heaviness of secrecy any longer, the husband confessed. His admission unleashed a storm. His wife's response moved in waves: sharp anger, deep sorrow, and finally a hollow sense of despair. For her, the betrayal wasn't just about the images, it was about the years of hiddenness, the walls erected between them, the intimacy quietly stolen.

And yet, in the ashes, a flicker of hope broke through. Their story was not one of instant healing, but of slow, painful rebuilding. It became a testimony to the power of confession, the necessity of grace, and the gritty reality that redemption often requires walking through fire together rather than around it.

Their healing journey was not linear, nor was it easy. But it was *deliberate*. They made the courageous choice to seek professional counseling, stepping into a space where raw emotions could be voiced without fear and where practical tools for recovery could be learned. Therapy became a place to name the addiction for what it was, to unravel its grip, and to begin rebuilding trust on the bedrock of honesty.

At the same time, they leaned heavily into prayer, not only the daily prayers of endurance, but times of inner healing prayer, where past wounds and lies could be exposed before the Lord. This spiritual dimension was essential; it reminded them that pornography wasn't exclusively a psychological struggle but a spiritual battle requiring divine intervention.

The church also became a lifeline. Brothers and sisters in Christ surrounded them with encouragement and accountability. They were not shamed but shepherded. The husband found a group of men who would ask the hard questions and refuse to let him slip back into secrecy. The wife found women who carried her burdens with compassion, helping her grieve, heal, and rediscover her worth.

Together, these layers, counseling, prayer, and community, wove a path toward restoration. Their marriage, though scarred, became stronger, more honest, and more dependent on God's grace than ever before.

Two years after that initial confession, the couple reflected on their journey with words that captured both their pain and their triumph: *"We're not back to what we were. We're better."*

That simple yet profound statement spoke volumes. Their marriage hadn't just been patched up or restored to some former state, it had been refined. What once was fractured by secrecy and shame had been rebuilt on radical honesty, shared vulnerability, and a renewed covenant of grace. They emerged not weaker but stronger, not defined by the scars of addiction but by the resilience that came through Christ's healing power.

Their story is a very vivid reminder that pornography, or any form of addiction, doesn't have to have the final word. With courage to face the truth, the humility to seek help, the support of a faith-filled community, and the relentless grace, marriages can not only survive but thrive. What the enemy meant for destruction, God can use for deeper intimacy, greater faith, and a testimony of hope.

The Kids Are Watching

Your conflict can be a classroom for your kids. Your children are watching you argue. They're learning how men respond to stress, how

Christians handle tension, and how husbands treat wives. If they see Dad say, "*I was wrong. Please forgive me,*" they learn humility. If they see Mom and Dad pray after a disagreement, they learn reconciliation. If they see shouting and sulking, they learn self-protection. Your marriage is shaping their theology.

Show Your Grace

Let your home be a school of grace. Teach your children what real love looks like: not conflict-free, but forgiveness-full. Not perfect harmony, but persistent unity. Let them see the gospel in how you say, "*I'm sorry,*" in how you hug after the storm, in how you refuse to give up on each other.

Men understand that conflict, while often uncomfortable, is not an enemy to be avoided. Instead, it is often a crucible in which true growth and strength are forged.

What you should truly fear is not the friction of disagreement, but the insidious decay that occurs when you retreat from necessary confrontation. Fear the suffocating silence that settles like a thick, visible mold overgrowing relationships, stifling communication and genuine connection. This silence is not peace; it is a vacuum where love and understanding wither.

Fear the hardened shell of pride that whispers deceptive assurances, convincing you, "*I don't need to change. I am sufficient as I am.*" This pride is a formidable barrier; it's preventing you from acknowledging your imperfections and embracing the transformative power of humility. It keeps you stagnant, unable to learn and evolve.

And most critically, fear the bitter root of unforgiveness and resentment that takes deep hold when emotional wounds are left unattended, festering in the dark corners of your heart. These unaddressed hurts breed a toxic acidity that corrodes your soul and damages your relationships from the inside out. They create walls, not bridges.

And above all, do not fear grace. Too often, we shrink from it as though it were dangerous, as though receiving undeserved mercy might cheapen our resolve. But grace is not a loophole for laziness. Grace is the ultimate game-changer, the divine catalyst that transforms everything.

It is the unmerited favor of God that dares to step into your mess, confront your shame, and lift you out of the pit you dug for yourself. Grace does what guilt never can: it gives you a future. It empowers you to forgive yourself and others. It frees you from the crushing weight of your past. It takes brokenness and rewrites it with redemption.

Grace doesn't wink at sin; it breaks sin's chains. It is the wellspring of real change, breathing life where death once ruled and shining light into the darkest corners of the soul. Embrace grace, really embrace it, and you will see how it rewrites your story into something far greater.

Marriage is not about finding someone who will never hurt you. It is about choosing to love someone when they don't. It is about fighting together, not just for peace, but for holiness. Where Christ is present, conflict becomes a canvas for the gospel. Where grace is chosen, marriages are healed, hearts are softened, and families are restored.

Alex and Maria

Alex and Maria had been married for seven years when Maria discovered a series of hurtful text messages between Alex and a female coworker. Though nothing physical had happened, the emotional intimacy felt like betrayal. Maria was crushed. Alex was defensive at first, but soon shame and regret settled in.

For weeks, their home felt cold. Meals were eaten in silence. Every conversation was cautious, like walking on broken glass. Maria wrestled with the idea that love meant staying, even when staying meant facing the person who had wounded her most. Alex wrestled with the realization that his sin had not only broken trust, but grieved God.

One night, they sat across from each other at the kitchen table. Alex uttered, voice trembling, *"I have sinned against you, and against the Lord. I don't deserve your forgiveness, but I'm asking for it."* Tears ran down Maria's face. At that moment, she chose not to end the marriage, but to start the hard work of rebuilding it.

There was no instant restoration. It took counseling, prayer, and months of small steps toward trust. But over time, the marriage that could have ended became a testimony of the gospel, where sin was met with confession, where pain was met with grace, and where Christ turned a wound into a witness.

So, when the next fight comes, and it will take a breath, say a prayer, and choose to walk through it, not around it. Choose humility over pride. Truth over silence. Grace over grit. And let Jesus, the ultimate reconciler, lead the way.

Reflection

- Identify one cultural or personal assumption about a woman's role that needs to be surrendered to Scripture's vision of honor and partnership.

- Confess all the ways you may have dismissed, silenced, or undervalued your wife's voice and gifting.

- Commit to a tangible act this week that affirms and supports her spiritual growth and flourishing.

- For singles/divorced/widowed: Identify how you can honor, encourage, and elevate the women God has placed in your life, whether family, friends, or church members, through words and actions that reflect Christ's example.

- Reflect on a real-life moment when you either succeeded or failed to honor a woman in your life and note what you learned for the future.

Prayer

Father, thank You for reconciling me to Yourself through Jesus. Teach me to steer with grace, humility, and sacrificial love. When conflict arises, give me patience. When I am hurt, give me mercy. When I fail, give me courage to repent. Let my life, and my relationships, be marked not by perfection, but by redemption. In Jesus' name, Amen.

Honoring Your Wife's Calling

"Husbands, live with your wives in an understanding way, showing honor to the woman as the weaker vessel, since they are heirs with you of the grace of life..." 1 Peter 3:7

One of the most damaging misconceptions in Christian marriage is the belief that the husband's mission is the only one that matters. This distortion often masquerades as biblical headship, but in reality, it undermines the very partnership God designed.

From the beginning, Scripture tells a different story. In Genesis 2, God declares,

"IT IS NOT GOOD THAT THE MAN SHOULD BE ALONE; I WILL MAKE HIM A HELPER FIT FOR HIM".

Eve's creation is not an afterthought or a subordinate add-on. It is a deliberate, divine act to complete what was otherwise *"not good."*

The Hebrew word for *"helper,"* ezer, shatters any attempt at shallow interpretations. It is the same word used throughout the Old Testament to describe God Himself as Israel's helper, *"Our soul waits for the Lord; he is our help (ezer) and our shield"*. This title speaks of strength, presence, and indispensable aid.

Far from implying inferiority, ezer conveys a role of power, partnership, and dignity. To diminish a wife's calling is to misrepresent God's own character, for He takes on the very name *"Helper"* with no hint of weakness.

When a husband grasps this truth, everything shifts. His wife is not a passive bystander to his calling, nor merely the support crew for his personal mission. She is a co-laborer in the work God has entrusted to them both. She is not a footnote in his story, but a headline in the narrative God is writing through their union.

Co-Heirs in Christ

To be *"co-heirs"* means husband and wife share the same spiritual inheritance. In Christ there is no hierarchy of worth. Both are image-bearers, redeemed by the same blood, filled with the same Spirit, and called into the same eternal mission.

Showing honor, then, is not mere courtesy, it is the deliberate act of elevating her God-given identity and affirming her dignity as an image-bearer of Christ.

When My Wife Went Back to School

Several years into our marriage, my wife told me she felt God stirring her heart to go back to school. She had put her dreams on hold for years to care for our family, but the desire never went away. When she first brought it up, I felt the weight of practical concerns. Tuition, schedules, childcare, all of it looked overwhelming. Part of me wanted to say no, not because I doubted her, but because I was afraid of the sacrifice it would require from both of us.

One night while praying, I came across Proverbs 31:28: *"Her children rise up and call her blessed; her husband also, and he praises her."* That verse hit me like a beam of light. If I wanted to live as a godly husband, I couldn't just allow her to follow God's call. I had to actively honor it.

So I shifted my perspective. I began looking for ways to support her instead of reasons to stop her. I picked up extra responsibilities around the house, rearranged my work schedule when I could, and made sure she had space to study without guilt. This wasn't always easy, but as she pressed forward, I saw her come alive in new ways.

Her confidence grew, her faith deepened, and our children watched their mother pursue her God-given calling with courage.

What Honor Looks Like

Honor is not passive. It is active. It looks like esteeming her not only in private but also in public, speaking well of her in the presence of others, defending her when necessary, and celebrating her victories as if they were your own. True honor does not shrink her, it enlarges her. It doesn't overshadow her; it shines a light on her.

Paul exhorts us:

"OUTDO ONE ANOTHER IN SHOWING HONOR."
ROMANS 12:10

That verse is often read in the context of church fellowship, but its first battleground is the home. For a husband, this is a radical call: to make honoring your wife not the exception, but the daily standard. Competing not for control, but for who can show greater Christlike esteem.

This honor begins first in the spiritual realm. A Christlike husband does not lead by authority alone, but by protecting the spiritual rhythms of the home.

He prays with and for his wife daily, covering her heart, her mind, and her calling with intercession. He actively encourages her pursuit of God, making sure she has the time, space, and freedom to cultivate her walk with Christ.

Her faith is not treated as an accessory to his leadership. It is honored as a vital, Spirit-filled force in their shared life.

A godly husband does not compete with her gifts or suppress them out of insecurity. Instead, he celebrates them. He supports the unique ways God has equipped her for kingdom impact, rejoicing as she flourishes.

Emotionally – Honor shows up as presence and attentiveness. It means listening without dismissing or rushing to fix, affirming her strengths, and walking patiently with her through struggles.

Practically – Honor shares burdens. It shows up in co-parenting, household partnership, serving willingly, and creating space for her to rest, dream, and flourish.

Publicly – Honor defends dignity. A husband refuses to tear down his wife through jokes, sarcasm, or criticism in front of others. Instead, he esteems her publicly, quotes her wisdom, and celebrates her victories as his own.

In contrast, a Christlike husband defends his wife's dignity in her absence. He highlights her strengths, quotes her wisdom, and refuses to entertain gossip or criticism. In doing so, he models the very love of Christ, who always covers, protects, and elevates His bride.

Honoring Her Calling

Her calling may take many forms, motherhood, business, education, ministry, counseling, art, or advocacy. There are no second-class callings in the kingdom.

True headship does not silence her calling; it makes space for it, champions it, and sacrifices for it. Sometimes that means shouldering extra responsibility, adjusting schedules, or tightening the budget so she can step into what God is asking of her.

Supporting a wife's calling does not diminish a husband's role or identity; it enriches both. When a husband champions his wife's God-given gifts, he is not stepping aside or losing ground. He is modeling Christlike love that seeks the good of another. In lifting her, he strengthens the marriage, because her flourishing adds to the joy and witness they share together. His leadership is not threatened but deepened, showing that true authority is never about control but about service and mutual growth.

This sacrifice is not weakness. It is strength, the strength of Christlike love that prioritizes her flourishing above convenience.

Jesus, in every encounter with women, lifted them higher.

Jesus as the Model

Jesus consistently elevated women.

- In John 4, He entrusted theological truth to the Samaritan woman, who became one of the first evangelists.
- In Luke 10, He praised Mary for choosing discipleship over cultural expectations.
- In Mark 5, He restored the bleeding woman's dignity, calling her "daughter" before the crowd.

In every encounter, Jesus affirmed women's worth and unleashed their potential. A godly husband reflects this same pattern.

In all these moments, Jesus honored their worth, affirmed their voice, and unleashed their potential. He did not silence women. He elevated them, restored them, and entrusted them with kingdom work.

When a husband chooses to honor his wife's calling, it will always cost him something. Sacrifice is part of the design.

There will be seasons when a husband must shoulder more of the household load so his wife can step into what God is calling her to do. Maybe it's leading a Bible study, pursuing seminary classes, or serving in ways that stretch the family's schedule.

Supporting her may mean tightening the budget to invest in her training. It may mean laying aside personal preferences to make room for her growth. It may mean choosing flexibility when her ministry to others requires time and energy.

This kind of sacrifice is not weakness, it is strength. It is the strength of Christlike love, the kind that puts her flourishing above your convenience, and her calling above your comfort.

None of this weakens your headship. It strengthens it. It mirrors the servant-hearted leadership of Christ. As Philippians 2:4 exhorts, "Let each of you look not only to his own interests, but also to the interests of others." A godly husband leads by lifting. He does not cling to comfort; he lays it down to see his wife flourish.

Some women, under the pressure of motherhood and the endless burdens of daily life, begin to lose sight of their God-ordained calling. They start to measure themselves only by what they do for others, rather than who they are in Christ.

This is where the husband's role becomes vital. He must speak life into her weary soul, reminding her of the truth: she is God's workmanship, created in Christ Jesus for good works prepared in advance for her to follow.

That kind of leadership is not tyranny. It is service. It dignifies, protects, and nurtures. It seeks the good of others, even at personal cost. Lived rightly, it becomes a shield of honor and a blessing.

He creates space for her to pause, to listen, and to rediscover her passions. In doing so, he helps her remember that she is more than her responsibilities. She is a daughter of the King, called and equipped for His purposes.

A godly husband does not stifle his wife's gifts but celebrates and cultivates them. If her heart beats for teaching, for writing, for mentoring younger women, or for launching a ministry or business, he champions her. This doesn't threaten biblical headship, it proves it.

Christ, our model, laid down His life to present His bride radiant and empowered. So too, a husband sacrifices his own comfort, convenience, and even preferences so that his wife can flourish in the calling God has placed on her life.

Real leadership does not require the spotlight. Sometimes it means applauding from behind the scenes. A man secure in his identity in Christ is not intimidated by his wife's success, wisdom, or strength. He sees her wins as their wins. He covers her in prayer, advocates for her voice, and softly corrects any lies she begins to believe about her worth or capacity.

In the end, honoring your wife's calling is not simply about supporting her dreams; it's about honoring the God who gave them to her. It is saying, "*I see the image of God in you, and I will do everything I can to help you live it out.*"

That kind of man reflects Christ. That kind of marriage changes families. And that kind of leadership rewrites legacies.

When a husband and wife mutually honor each other's callings, a powerful spiritual dynamic is released in the home. Children raised in such an environment see faith not as a rigid set of rules, but as a living, breathing reality.

They grow up witnessing the beauty of collaboration, the strength of sacrifice, and the power of a love that mirrors Christ and His Church. Ministry multiplies, not because one person is elevated above the other, but because both are running their race with encouragement, humility, and unity.

In a world that often diminishes or distorts the role of women, the Christian husband is called to display something radical and redemptive: a love that honors, a leadership that uplifts, and a partnership that reflects the very heart of God. This is the kind of marriage that glorifies Christ, transforms homes, and leaves a legacy of faith for generations yet to come.

Modern Examples

Consider David and Esther Platt. While David is widely recognized as a pastor and author, Esther has faithfully pursued her own calling in discipleship and hospitality. She has led Bible studies for young women, mentored others, and quietly shaped lives behind the scenes. David has often spoken about how her ministry not only enriches their marriage but also extends their reach, bringing wisdom and perspective where his gifts may not.

Their impact is not the product of one mission overshadowing the other, but the strength of a shared pursuit. Together, they display the beauty of a partnership where both callings are honored and leveraged for kingdom purposes.

Or take the case of Lecrae and his wife, Darragh. Lecrae carries a public ministry through music and advocacy, while Darragh has poured her life into homeschooling their children and championing initiatives for foster care and adoption. Lecrae consistently acknowledges her as a true co-laborer, pointing to her discernment and courage as essential to their shared mission.

Their marriage illustrates that honoring callings does not require identical roles, but equal value and respect for the roles God assigns.

Even in the corporate world, Christian couples are modeling this principle. In 2022, *Forbes* profiled Jeff and Brittany Martin, co-founders of *Collective*, a faith-driven networking group for young professionals.

Jeff, once a sports agent, now leads strategy and outreach. Brittany, a gifted designer and speaker, stewards the creative and formational side of the company. Their callings are different, but they are not divided. Together they testify that honoring one another's gifts sharpens both their marriage and their mission.

Their story reminds us that this principle is not confined to the pulpit or the home. It extends into every sphere where men and women live out their God-given assignments. When a husband and wife choose to support rather than suppress one another's callings, the impact multiplies.

And this brings us to the next truth: honoring one another's gifts is not about personal fulfillment, it is about kingdom effectiveness. It is about reflecting the complementary design of God in marriage and in mission.

Across ministry, family, and business, these couples show the same truth: when husbands and wives choose to honor each other's calling, their partnership becomes stronger, their witness broader, and their legacy deeper.

These examples reflect a key biblical truth: God does not call one spouse to flourish at the expense of the other. When both husband and wife walk in their God-given purposes, the whole household thrives. Children see faith as a dynamic force, not a hierarchical script. Communities are blessed, ministries are birthed, and Christ is glorified.

The Cost of Honor and Its Fruit

Honoring your wife's calling will cost you something, time, convenience, ego. But the fruit far outweighs the sacrifice.

A secure man is not threatened by his wife's success. He applauds it, prays over it, and sees her wins as their wins. He reminds her of her worth when she forgets, creating a home where her gifts are cultivated and her calling affirmed.

In the end, honoring your wife's calling is about honoring the God who gave it. When husbands and wives both flourish, their marriage becomes a testimony of Christ and His Church, a partnership that glorifies God, blesses communities, and leaves a legacy of faith for generations.

Ask your wife what dream God has put on her heart. Then ask how you can practically support it this week

Reflection

- Identify one way you've treated your wife's calling as secondary and confess it to God.

- Acknowledge specific gifts or dreams your wife carries that you have overlooked or minimized.

- Commit to one concrete action this week that affirms and supports her God-given purpose.

- Envision how your leadership could reflect Christ more fully by consistently honoring her.

Prayer

Father, thank You for the gift of my wife and the calling You've placed on her life. Help me to lead with humility, listen with understanding, and honor her with my words and actions. Forgive me for the times I've overlooked or dismissed her gifts. Teach me to champion her purpose with joy, so that together we may walk in Your grace. In Jesus' name, Amen.

Fatherhood with Purpose

"Fathers, do not provoke your children to anger, but bring them up in the discipline and instruction of the Lord." Ephesians 6:4

A Generation in Crisis

Our generation is living through a fatherhood crisis. But fatherhood is no accident. It is not a side role or biological footnote. It is a sacred assignment designed by God to reflect His own character.

"AS A FATHER SHOWS COMPASSION TO HIS CHILDREN, SO THE LORD
SHOWS COMPASSION TO THOSE WHO FEAR HIM"
PSALM 103:13.

The heart of God is revealed in the heart of a father. That means our calling extends far beyond paying the bills or setting boundaries. It is a commission to shape souls, to nourish identity, and to lay down a spiritual foundation that will endure for generations. It is to live as men who embody compassion, consistency, and covenant love, the very attributes of our Heavenly Father.

The good news is this: no matter your past, no matter the failures of your own father or even your personal shortcomings, the grace of God can redeem and reshape your story. In Christ, you are not left to father in your own strength. You are equipped by the Spirit, anchored in the Word, and guided by the example of your Heavenly Father.

Where some say fathers don't matter, Scripture proclaims the opposite. Where brokenness marks our stories, God offers restoration. In Christ, we are equipped by His Spirit, anchored in His Word, and called to raise disciples who see in us a reflection of the Father who never fails.

Four Roles of a Father

Scripture offers a rich vision for fatherhood. A father is:

Protector – shielding his home from harm, both physical and spiritual.

Provider – offering not only income, but wisdom, security, and presence.

Priest – leading the family in worship, prayer, and obedience to God's Word.

Pattern – modeling integrity, humility, repentance, and faith for his children to follow.

"THE RIGHTEOUS WHO WALKS IN HIS INTEGRITY, BLESSED ARE HIS
CHILDREN AFTER HIM!"
PROVERBS 20:7

A father's influence outlives him. His daily choices either become a stumbling block or a steppingstone for his children's faith.

Living Sermons

Children often act as sponges, absorbing not only the words we speak, but more significantly, the silent lessons of our daily existence. Our lectures, though well-intended, may fade from their memories, yet the vivid tapestry of our lives, our actions, reactions, and the very spirit we embody remains permanently etched.

It is this consistent, lived example that serves as the most potent architect of their worldview and shapes the bedrock of their values.

Consider the profound impact of a father who is slow to anger. In a world often characterized by impulsive reactions and volatile emotions, his calm demeanor becomes a tangible lesson in patience. His children witness firsthand the strength in restraint, the wisdom in measured responses, and the profound peace that stems from self-control. They learn that true power lies not in an outburst, but in the deliberate choice to remain composed, even in the face of provocation.

When a father demonstrates the courage to confess his sin openly, he dismantles the formidable wall of shame and secrecy that so often surrounds failure. Instead of hiding behind silence or masking weakness with pride, he steps into the light. This act of vulnerability, far from diminishing his authority, elevates him as a beacon of authenticity.

Children who witness this kind of humility encounter something deeply countercultural. They live in a world where most men cover, excuse, or justify their failings. Yet when they see their father kneel before God and admit, *"I was wrong, please forgive me,"* they are being discipled into the reality of grace.

Repentance becomes more than a theological concept; it becomes flesh and blood before their eyes. They learn that mistakes, while painful, are not fatal. They discover that brokenness is not the end, but an invitation to restoration.

His children grasp that God does not require perfection to love us, but a humble and contrite heart. They see that true strength is not found in flawless performance, but in courageous humility. They begin to understand that repentance is not weakness, it is the doorway to freedom, growth, and renewed intimacy with both God and family.

The way a father treats their mother speaks volumes, resonating far beyond any verbal instruction. Children are always watching, even when they pretend not to. Every act of tenderness, every word of honor, and every demonstration of respect becomes a silent sermon that shapes their vision of love.

When a father constantly treats his wife with honor, respect, and deep affection, he is doing more than being a good husband. He is shaping the spiritual imagination of his children.

They watch him and learn what covenantal love looks like in flesh and blood. They see what it means to cherish another human being, to value her voice, and to protect her dignity.

It happens in the everyday moments. When Dad chooses patience instead of sarcasm. When he celebrates Mom's strengths instead of competing with them. When he prays with her instead of dismissing her concerns.

In those choices, his children are receiving a living education in Christlike love, an education that will echo in their own marriages and families for generations to come.

This is why Paul's exhortation in Ephesians carries such weight. The father who embodies sacrificial love toward his wife is not only obeying Scripture; he is building a legacy. His children internalize the importance of mutual esteem, equitable partnership, and the sacred bond of marriage.

That lived example becomes their blueprint. Sons grow up learning that real strength is expressed through gentleness and humility. Daughters grow up knowing their worth is immeasurable and should never be compromised for shallow affection. Together, they carry forward the conviction that the sacred bond of marriage flourishes where love is nurtured, honor is practiced, and grace is abundant.

And perhaps most importantly, when a father regularly places God first in his life, he provides his children with an enduring compass for their own spiritual journey.

His devotion is not measured merely by Sunday attendance, but by the quiet consistency of prayer, the integrity of his decisions, and the way his priorities clearly point to Christ. His children see, day after day, that faith is not a compartment of life but the very foundation upon which all else is built.

This unwavering devotion, manifested in his time, his choices, and his humble reverence, communicates the profound weight of faith. They come to understand that there is a higher authority, a guiding light, and an ultimate source of truth and purpose beyond themselves.

Deuteronomy captures this vision:

> *"AND THESE WORDS THAT I COMMAND YOU TODAY SHALL BE ON YOUR HEART. YOU SHALL TEACH THEM DILIGENTLY TO YOUR CHILDREN AND SHALL TALK OF THEM WHEN YOU SIT IN YOUR HOUSE, AND WHEN YOU WALK BY THE WAY, AND WHEN YOU LIE DOWN, AND WHEN YOU RISE."*
> *DEUTERONOMY 6:6–7*

A father who lives this out shows his children that reverence is not a rigid rule, but a heartfelt response to the God who loves and leads.

In essence, our lives become the living sermons our children cannot ignore. They may forget a lecture, they may resist a command, but they will never forget a life authentically surrendered to Christ. That example becomes their compass, orienting them toward the One who is "the way, the truth, and the life".

A 2023 national study revealed that children whose fathers modeled regular prayer and engagement with Scripture were more likely to remain in the faith as adults. (Zammit, 2023) Faithfulness, not perfection, is what leaves a legacy. There are two ditches that provoke children to anger: harshness and absence.

- Harshness – Constant criticism, unrealistic demands, or angry outbursts crush a child's spirit. Outward compliance may result, but inward discouragement festers.

- Absence – A father may live at home yet remain emotionally distant. Children interpret absence as rejection, opening doors to insecurity and searching for validation elsewhere.

Even culture recognizes the difference.

Real Dads

NBA star Jimmy Butler speaks of the pain of abandonment. In contrast, actor Denzel Washington often credits his father's presence for shaping his values. Faithful fatherhood is about presence, showing up with consistency, gentleness, and strength.

Another example is Denzel Washington, who has spoken about the importance of his father's presence in shaping his values and spiritual life. When asked what it is that's missing in modern communities, Denzel pointed to the absence of strong fathers. He emphasized that a man doesn't have to be perfect to make a difference, he simply has to show up.

Faithful fatherhood is about more than providing. It's about presence. It's about guiding with gentleness and leading with strength. It's about praying over your children when they sleep and speaking life over them when they fail. It's about putting down your phone to look them in the eyes, asking hard questions, and being brave enough to admit when you're wrong.

Dads Lesson

Mark had always promised himself he would be a better father than his own dad. But as the pressures of work mounted, the long hours and constant stress left him drained by the time he walked through the front door. His son, Caleb, would run up with excitement, toy in hand, ready to play. Too often, Mark brushed him off with a tired "Not now." When Caleb's shoulders slumped and he walked away, Mark told himself he would make it up to him another day.

One evening, after another long day, Mark walked past Caleb's room and overheard him telling his mother, "Dad's always too busy for me." The words hit him like a blow. He realized that the same wounds he carried from his own father's absence were the very ones he was now passing on.

For the first time, Mark admitted to himself that he was failing. He sat down with Caleb, looked him in the eyes, and said, "Son, I've been wrong. I've been too focused on work and not enough on you. I want to change. Will you forgive me?" Caleb hesitated at first but then nodded and leaned into his father's arms.

Growth did not happen overnight. Mark had to reorder his priorities. He began leaving work earlier at least twice a week, dedicating that time to his family. He started small, helping with homework, tossing a ball in the yard, praying with Caleb before bed. Slowly, their bond began to heal.

Mark learned that fatherhood was not about perfection but about presence. Failure did not have to be the last word. By confessing his weakness and choosing to grow, he discovered that God's grace could redeem even his shortcomings. In the very place where he once fell short, he became a stronger, more loving father.

Time for Revival

Modern fatherhood needs a revival. Not of dominance or control, but of godly leadership rooted in humility, courage, and grace. We need more dads who hug first, apologize first, and pray first. Fathers who model repentance, resilience, and reverence for God.

In doing so, they won't just raise well-behaved kids, they'll raise image-bearers who know they are loved by both their earthly father and their Heavenly One.

On the other hand, absence leaves children adrift. A father may be physically in the home but emotionally unavailable. He may prioritize work, hobbies, or screens over meaningful connection. He may delegate all spiritual leadership to his wife or church, failing to engage personally in the spiritual development of his children. Absence breeds insecurity, while harshness breeds rebellion. But love, consistency, and presence create confidence.

Discipline That Restores

Discipline is not a form of punishment; it is a form of discipleship. Hebrews 12:6 reminds us that "the Lord disciplines those He loves."

Discipline, when done biblically, does not aim to crush a child's spirit but to guide them back to the truth. It starts with the father's self-control, seeks restoration rather than retribution, and ends with reconnection.

A father who disciplines like Christ prioritizes his child's heart over mere outward behavior. His approach to correction is rooted in empathy and instruction, transforming moments of discipline into profound teaching opportunities. This Christ-like discipline mirrors the divine love and patience, aiming not just to correct actions but to cultivate a righteous character from within.

The parable of the Prodigal Son in Luke 15 offers one of the clearest pictures of a father's redemptive posture. Even after the younger son had squandered his inheritance and abandoned his home, the father was not fixated on the rebellion, the shame, or the wasted years. Instead, he remained watchful, waiting with a heart full of compassion. When he finally saw his son in the distance, he did not fold his arms in cold judgment, he ran to him. He embraced him. He restored him fully into the family, clothing him with honor and covering him with unconditional love.

Discipline must follow that pattern, truth that names sin, and grace that opens the way back. Such correction not only shapes behavior but also instills hope, teaching children that a father's love, and God's love, never fails.

Leading Spiritually

One of the greatest and most sacred privileges of fatherhood is the call to usher your children into the presence of God. This is not a responsibility to outsource or a role to passively hope someone else will fill. Rather, it is a divine mandate woven into the very fabric of fatherhood itself, a sacred mantle entrusted by God to you.

As fathers, we are called to be the primary spiritual guides of our homes. This means that fatherhood is not just about passing along Bible verses, but about living a faith so genuine and vibrant that your children see it, feel it, and long to imitate it.

Leading spiritually means:

- Praying with them daily.

- Reading Scripture aloud and letting them see you wrestle with it.

- Worshiping as a family at church and at home.

- Serving together, showing compassion in action.

True leadership means allowing your reverence for God to permeate every corner of daily life. How you work. How you rest. How you treat others.

When children see this, they learn that faith is not a compartment, neatly tucked into Sundays. It is a compass, steady and sure, guiding every step.

When a father embraces this sacred calling, his home becomes a living sanctuary, a place where God's Word is cherished, His presence is sought, and His love is experienced. Few legacies are more enduring than this: raising children who do not simply know about God, but who have been led by their father to walk with Him personally.

Begin by reading Scripture together. You don't need a theology degree. Open the Bible, read a few verses, and ask questions. Let your children hear your voice speak God's Word over them. Pray together daily. Let them hear your heart cry out to God, for their fears, their dreams, and their future. Worship as a family, both at church and at home. Make reverence normal.

Also, serve together. Whether it's volunteering at a shelter, visiting a lonely neighbor, or mowing a widow's lawn, show them that love looks like action. James 1:27 reminds us that pure religion is caring for orphans and widows. Let your children see compassion in motion.

Words of Blessing

Every child longs to hear three things:

I love you.
I'm proud of you.
You have what it takes.

At Jesus' baptism, the Father declared:

"THIS IS MY BELOVED SON, IN WHOM I AM WELL PLEASED"
MATTHEW 3:17.

Before Jesus had performed miracles, He was already affirmed. Fathers are called to echo this blessing, privately, sincerely, and even publicly.

Our children often look to us for validation and guidance, even when they don't explicitly ask for it. It's crucial not to assume they inherently know the depth of your love and pride. Instead, make a conscious effort to verbalize these feelings regularly.

Speak your affection and affirmation often. These aren't sentiments to be reserved for special occasions; they should be woven into the fabric of daily life. A simple "*I love you*" or "*I'm proud of you*" can resonate strongly and build their self-esteem.

Crucially, speak it sincerely. Children are perceptive and can often discern insincerity. Let your words be genuine, reflecting the true emotions of your heart. When your words align with your actions, your message gains power and authenticity.

Finally, speak it publicly. While private affirmations are vital, there's a unique power in hearing a parent's blessing spoken in front of others. This public declaration reinforces their worth, demonstrates your unwavering support, and can instill a profound sense of security and purpose.

Your verbal blessing, consistently and sincerely delivered, has the remarkable ability to shape their self-perception, fuel their aspirations, and ultimately set a positive trajectory for their entire lives.

Stories of Restoration

For fathers carrying regret, hear this: it's never too late. Malachi 4:6 promises that God will turn hearts of fathers to children.

In 2024, a man in his sixties reconciled with his estranged son through handwritten letters of humility. Over time, silence gave way to conversation, bitterness to forgiveness, distance to prayer. His legacy, almost lost, was redeemed by grace.

Restoration rarely comes in one dramatic moment. It comes through small, steady steps of humility and prayer. But God delights to bring beauty from ashes.

Today, they attend church together. The son brings his own children. And that father, once estranged, now lays hands on his grandchildren and prays blessing over them. His legacy, almost lost, was reclaimed by grace.

Modern Models of Fatherhood

Benjamin Watson, known to many for his years as an NFL tight end, stands as a strong modern picture of biblical fatherhood. His professional life demanded relentless training, exhausting travel, and the constant pressure of performing under bright lights.

Yet even in the chaos of athletic fame, Watson was unshakably clear about what mattered most. His greatest title was never *"NFL veteran,"* but *"Dad."*

Whether speaking openly about the sanctity of life, the responsibility of fathers, or the beauty of raising his seven children with his wife Kirsten, Watson has consistently modeled a truth our broken world desperately needs: manhood is not measured by trophies or contracts, but by the faithfulness with which a man loves, protects, and shepherds his family.

As Watson poignantly reminds us: "Dads don't babysit. They parent."

In his witness, Watson exemplifies that true manhood isn't measured by trophies or headlines, but by the faithful love, protective strength, and spiritual leadership one offers to his family.

What makes his testimony remarkable is not simply his words, but his visible example. Pictures of him reading Scripture with his kids, leading family devotions, or simply celebrating their milestones remind us that a father's influence is not measured by career success but by daily faithfulness at home. In Watson's life, we see a clear portrait of Psalm 127:3 lived out: *"Children are a heritage from the Lord, offspring a reward from him."*

Benjamin Watson's example challenges every Christian father to reconsider where their priorities lie. True legacy is not left in trophies or accolades, but in the spiritual seeds planted in the next generation. His life underscores this truth: the most significant victories a man will ever achieve are not on the field or in the workplace, but in the hearts of the children he is called to shepherd.

Watson emphasized that fatherhood is far more than financial provision. It is the sacred work of shaping souls.

For him, intentional time, discipleship, and prayer within the home formed the cornerstone of parenting. He carved out space for presence, not just productivity.

He read Scripture with his children, not as a hollow ritual, but as a deliberate act of formation. He wanted them immersed in the truth of God, able to see the world through a biblical lens, equipped to discern right from wrong.

Anchoring your Kids

In this, Watson modeled a father's highest calling: to anchor his children in Christ amid an increasingly secular world, preparing them to stand firm long after his own voice is gone.

His example underscores the profound influence a father can wield when he invests in his children's spiritual formation. Even during a demanding public career, Watson demonstrated that faith and family must remain paramount. His life challenges us to ask: are we merely providing for our children's needs, or are we also shepherding their souls?

In 2023, a video of a father named Joe Mullins went viral. He stood outside his son's school every morning holding a sign that read, "*You are loved. You are enough. You are mine.*" His son had struggled with bullying and anxiety, and instead of minimizing the issue, this dad met it head-on with presence, encouragement, and visible love. That small act of faithfulness brought healing and security to his child and inspired countless others to do the same.

Another example is Jason Romano, a former ESPN producer who left his high-profile media job to focus on ministry and family. He now leads Sports Spectrum; a ministry focused on the intersection of faith and sports and frequently speaks on the role of Christian fathers. His decision to choose calling over comfort became a role model to his children about the importance of obedience to God.

An Awakening

In the quiet town of Willow Creek, Indiana, a profound spiritual awakening began to stir in 2022. At the center was Pastor Mark Farlow, shepherd of Willow Creek Community Church.

As he watched his congregation, Farlow noticed a troubling pattern. Young fathers were weary; their faith pushed to the margins by the relentless demands of work and family. They were good men, devoted to providing, yet adrift spiritually. Their energy was depleted, their compass clouded.

Rather than ignore what he saw, Pastor Farlow leaned in. His compassion and foresight would become the spark that set something far greater in motion.

Driven by a deep conviction to equip men for their divine calling as godly husbands and fathers, Pastor Farlow launched a humble yet bold initiative he called *"Dad Discipleship."* The beginning was anything but glamorous. There were no banners, no polished programs, and no committees drafting vision statements. Instead, the inaugural gathering took place in the familiar, oil-scented comfort of his own garage. Four men showed up that night, ordinary dads with extraordinary hunger.

Each man clutched a steaming mug of coffee in one hand and a well-worn Bible in the other. They gathered on folding chairs in a garage that still smelled faintly of motor oil. Wrenches lay scattered across the workbench. A couple of bikes leaned against the wall. Just an ordinary space, yet at that moment it became a sanctuary.

There, in the middle of tools and clutter, something sacred began to stir. Vulnerability broke through the silence as one after another admitted struggles, confessed fears, and spoke of the deep longing to lead their families well.

Together, they opened the Scriptures. Not as detached scholars, but as desperate fathers. Their prayers weren't polished; their reading wasn't rehearsed. They were pleading, pleading for wisdom, courage, and grace.

What began as a quiet experiment in discipleship soon grew into a movement. Within a year, more than thirty fathers had joined, a clear sign of the deep spiritual hunger stirring among men who longed to be equipped for their God-ordained role.

The garage, once reserved for tools and weekend projects, had been transformed. It was no longer just a place of work but a sanctuary of prayer, study, and brotherhood.

Week after week, the men gathered with one aim. They prayed fervently for their children. They anchored their lives in the timeless truths of God's Word. They held one another accountable, pushing each other toward authentic faith, not only within their homes but also throughout their neighborhoods.

This was never about programs or polish. The purpose was to be present. In a world where fatherhood is often diminished, *Dad Discipleship* reclaimed it as holy ground. And in that ordinary garage, heaven touched earth through the prayers of fathers who refused to drift into passivity, choosing instead to embrace their calling as spiritual leaders.

Pastor Farlow's quiet obedience to God's prompting, his willingness to start small and serve faithfully, has yielded an impact far beyond the four walls of his garage. What began with four men around a workbench has become a movement shaping dozens of homes. The transformation unfolding within these fathers is not merely personal; it is profoundly generational.

Each man who kneels in prayer for his children, who learns to confess sin openly, and who leads his home with humility and strength is planting seeds that will outlast him. Sons are learning firsthand what it means to be godly men. Daughters are watching what it looks like to be cherished and honored. Families once fractured by neglect or passivity are finding stability in Christ.

This is the beauty of multiplication in the kingdom of God. One pastor's faithful "*yes*" created a sanctuary out of a garage and sparked a renewal in the hearts of fathers who were desperate to lead well. And the ripples are spreading still, through children, grandchildren, and communities touched by the overflow of transformed homes.

It is living proof that the smallest acts of faith, an invitation, a gathering, a prayer whispered in obedience, can ignite movements for the glory of God.

Whether you're a blue-collar worker, an executive, or a stay-at-home dad, the principle remains the same: faithfulness in fatherhood matters. When you kneel to pray over your children, heaven listens. When you repent for your failures and ask your child's forgiveness, you model grace. When you show up to every game, concert, and difficult conversation, you are reflecting the faithfulness of the God who never misses a moment.

In a culture increasingly marked by absent fathers and spiritual confusion, your role as a godly dad is more critical than ever. You are not just raising sons and daughters, you are raising future husbands, wives, leaders, and disciples. You are shaping eternity one bedtime story, one prayer, and one act of sacrificial love at a time.

Legacy That Lasts

Nearly one in four children—about 18.4 million—live without a father in the home in the U.S. (Kramer, 2019)

The need is urgent.

But faithful fatherhood is not being perfect. It is presence. It is repentance. It is prayer. It is sowing seeds of grace in ordinary days.

Fatherhood is not about raising compliant kids but raising image-bearers who know the love of their earthly father and their Heavenly Father.

So, fathers, be present. Be prayerful. Be men after God's own heart. And trust this: the seeds you sow in faith will bear fruit in due season.

Reflection

- Identify the legacy you are intentionally, or unintentionally, building for your children.

- Evaluate whether you are emotionally present, not just physically available.

- Examine what your discipline communicates, does it model grace, or instill fear?

- Commit to reflecting God the Father in the way you love, correct, and lead your home.

Prayer

Father God, thank You for being the perfect Father. Teach me to love, lead, and serve my children with Your heart. Forgive me for failing and strengthen me for this calling. Let my words build, my discipline and let my life reflect Christ. May my children see and know You more because of how I father them. In Jesus' name, Amen.

Legacy and the Long View

"A good man leaves an inheritance to his children's children..."
Proverbs 13:22

Let's set the record straight: legacy is not your retirement fund, your name etched on a brick in the church courtyard, or the number of casseroles served at your funeral reception. It's not about the car you hand down or the applause you collected in the office. Those things are temporary, fading as quickly as the next economic cycle or the next generation's priorities.

Real legacy, the kind that echoes into eternity, is not what you leave *for* your children, it is what you leave *in* them. It is the spiritual DNA woven into their souls, the unshakable convictions you model, the daily patterns of truth, grace, strength, and presence they witness in your life. Long after your body returns to dust, those imprints remain.

And here's the sobering reality: whether you like it or not, you are leaving a legacy. Everyone does. Every word you speak, every choice you make, every priority you establish in your home is planting seeds. The only question is whether yours will be worth repeating or desperately needing to be undone.

The Apostle Paul, with piercing clarity, sets the standard:

"ONLY LET YOUR MANNER OF LIFE BE WORTHY OF THE GOSPEL OF CHRIST."
PHILIPPIANS 1:27

This is not a suggestion, but a summons. It transcends fleeting opinion, shifting cultural tides, or even the habits passed down from your father's household. It demands that the story your children inherit from you aligns with the eternal story of redemption, sacrifice, and hope found in Christ.

Legacy is not optional. The only question is: will it point your children toward Christ, or away from Him?

Legacy Is Built in the Trenches

The concept of legacy, often perceived as a distant future aspiration, is in fact a present reality. It doesn't begin "*later*" when we've achieved some arbitrary milestone; it commences "*now*." Its birthplace is in the demanding "*trenches*" of daily life. This means that the genuine measure of our legacy is found in the seemingly mundane, yet deeply significant, interactions and choices we make every single day.

Consider how you navigate the chaos of the morning rush. Do you meet it with calm and patience, or with frustration and sharp words that wound more than you realize? When exhaustion has drained your reserves and the veneer of civility is stripped away, what remains? What kind of husband are you when the world isn't watching, when the only witnesses are your wife, your children, and your own conscience?

Do your actions toward your wife consistently reflect love, respect, and selflessness, or do they reveal neglect, indifference, or entitlement? And perhaps most tellingly, what role does God's Word play in your life? Is your Bible a neglected relic, collecting dust as a silent witness to your spiritual apathy? Or is it a well-loved companion, its pages worn, margins filled with notes, and heart truths pressed into your soul from frequent study and earnest prayer?

These are the moments, the habits, the choices that weave the fabric of your legacy. Legacy is not crafted in grand gestures but in the hidden faithfulness of daily life. It is forged in the patience shown when anger could have erupted, in the prayers whispered when worry pressed in, in the quiet honoring of your wife when no one else was watching.

Make no mistake, this fabric will not remain neutral. It will either fray and unravel with time, leaving only regret, or it will endure as a garment of righteousness. And when it endures, it becomes something greater than yourself, handed down as a covering for your children and their children, a legacy that honors Christ long after you are gone.

Hidden Faithfulness, Eternal Impact

Consider the story of Susanna Wesley, the mother of John and Charles Wesley. She never preached a sermon, published a book, or led a revival. Instead, she faithfully taught her children at the kitchen table, read Scripture aloud, and prayed over them daily.

Her hidden faithfulness became the soil from which two of the most influential ministers in church history grew. John himself once said, *"I learned more about Christianity from my mother than from all the theologians in England."* Susanna's legacy was not a monument but a model, ordinary devotion, extraordinary impact.

In the same way, fathers today must remember that their children will likely forget much of what was bought for them. The gifts will fade, the toys will be replaced, the clothes will wear out.

But they will not forget the atmosphere they grew up in. Was it marked by prayer and peace? By Christlike love and stability? Or was it marked by tension, neglect, and hypocrisy?

Paul reminded Timothy that faith itself can be a generational inheritance:

"I AM REMINDED OF YOUR SINCERE FAITH, A FAITH THAT DWELT FIRST IN YOUR GRANDMOTHER LOIS AND YOUR MOTHER EUNICE AND

NOW, I AM SURE, DWELLS IN YOU AS WELL"
2 TIMOTHY 1:5.

Your children and grandchildren may one day say the same of you. Or they may spend years trying to heal from what you failed to pass down.

Legacy is not a "someday" idea. It is today's reality. The small things you do, or don't do, are writing a story. And that story is either pointing to Christ or something much smaller.

Faith That Echoes Through Generations

Consider Abraham. The man didn't just believe God. He uprooted his life based on a promise and became the patriarch of faith. Genesis records God's words:

"I WILL MAKE OF YOU A GREAT NATION, AND I WILL BLESS YOU AND MAKE YOUR NAME GREAT, SO THAT YOU WILL BE A BLESSING... IN YOU ALL THE FAMILIES OF THE EARTH SHALL BE BLESSED."
GENESIS 12:2–3

That's a legacy that moved history. He didn't just live well. He believed well.

Abraham's faith wasn't a sentimental gesture. It was bold, disruptive obedience. He left behind familiarity, comfort, and security for the unknown, not because he had all the answers, but because he trusted the One who did. God reminds us,

"BY FAITH ABRAHAM OBEYED WHEN HE WAS CALLED TO GO OUT TO A PLACE THAT HE WAS TO RECEIVE AS AN INHERITANCE. AND HE WENT OUT, NOT KNOWING WHERE HE WAS GOING."
HEBREWS 11:8

That kind of faith leaves fingerprints on generations. Abraham didn't just pass on sheep and land; he passed on a vision of trust in God. His legacy wasn't in what he built but in who he believed. Every spiritual father, every man of faith today stands in the shadow of his obedience.

David's epitaph was simple:

"DAVID SERVED THE PURPOSE OF GOD IN HIS OWN GENERATION"
ACTS 13:36.

His psalms still fuel millions today.

Paul didn't leave legacy to chance. He commanded Timothy to entrust truth to faithful men who would teach others also. That's intentional multiplication.

Billy Graham lived this too. His crusades drew millions, but his real genius was training leaders through the Lausanne Movement and his Evangelistic Association. His discipleship ripples still today.

He understood what Paul modeled, that the mission outlives the man when discipleship is intentional. The men and women he trained continue to impact nations decades after his voice first filled stadiums.

Legacy is not just what you leave behind. It is who you send forward.

Legacy in Denim: Everyday Discipleship

A 2019 Barna study confirmed what Scripture has always declared: children raised in homes where Christianity was lived with joy and authenticity, not just preached, were five times more likely to remain in the faith. (Barna, 2019) This reinforces what Scripture has always declared: faith that is embodied is faith that endures.

This remarkable finding is not mystical or coincidental. It is a testament to the tangible, transformative power of everyday discipleship, what I like to call *"discipleship in denim."* This phrase captures the essence of faith formation in the ordinary: jeans and t-shirts, family dinners, car rides, bedtime prayers, and backyard conversations. It is not about perfection, polish, or the performance of religion. It is about faith woven into the fabric of real life.

This is where children learn the gospel not as theory but as reality. They see Dad pray in moments of stress. They hear Mom sing praise while folding laundry. They watch their parents resolve conflict with grace. They feel the burden of Scripture applied to the ups and downs of daily living.

These lived examples plant seeds that sermons alone cannot. They etch into memory the truth that Christianity is not a Sunday-only event, but a 24/7 way of life.

Men, your voice matters. Say what needs to be said. Not just when it's easy. Say, *"I love you,"* when it feels awkward. Say, *"I'm proud of you,"* when your son screws up but comes back. Don't assume they know. Tell them. Repeatedly.

Jesus's teachings serve as a profound call to re-evaluate our priorities and shift our focus from the temporal to the eternal. He wasn't merely offering advice; He was delivering a direct, unmistakable truth about the futility of chasing worldly possessions:

"DO NOT STORE UP FOR YOURSELVES TREASURES ON EARTH, WHERE MOTHS AND VERMIN DESTROY, AND WHERE THIEVES BREAK IN AND STEAL. BUT STORE UP FOR YOURSELVES TREASURES IN HEAVEN, WHERE MOTHS AND VERMIN DO NOT DESTROY, AND WHERE THIEVES DO NOT BREAK IN AND STEAL."
MATTHEW 6:19–20

This passage is not confined to the narrow scope of money or material wealth; it reaches into every area of life. Anything we cling to that cannot endure, status, comfort, reputation, or even achievements, will one day fade. The houses we build will crumble, the trophies will tarnish, the bank accounts will empty. What remains, what carries eternal weight, are the lives we touch, the faith we model, and the legacy we invest in the next generation.

Jesus draws a stark line: the things of this world are fragile, vulnerable to decay and theft. But the investments we make into the kingdom of God, discipleship, acts of love, sacrifices of obedience, prayers whispered in faith, are indestructible. They are treasures secured in heaven's vaults, immune to the erosion of time or the schemes of the enemy.

For fathers, husbands, and leaders, this truth reframes the question of legacy. The real measure of our lives is not what we *leave behind* in material terms, but what we *send ahead* into eternity. Every time we disciple a child, honor our wife, speak truth with integrity, or model Christ in the mundane details of daily life, we are depositing treasure where it will never be lost.

Eternal Investments, Not Junk That Burns

The "*junk that burns*" isn't limited to money or possessions. It encompasses anything we invest our lives in that lacks eternal value. This could be fleeting fame, transient pleasures, self-serving ambitions, or even excessive devotion to hobbies or careers that don't ultimately serve a higher purpose. These are the things that, like hay and stubble, will be consumed by the fires of eternity, leaving nothing but ash.

In stark contrast, Jesus urges us to "*Lay up treasures in heaven.*" This is where true and lasting riches are found. These treasures are not tangible; they are spiritual and relational. They are the investments we make in God's kingdom and in the lives of others, especially those within our own homes.

"That includes people, especially your own household." This is a critical emphasis. Our families, our spouses, children, and even extended relatives are not merely obligations but divine trusts. The time, love, attention, and prayers we pour into them are not wasted; they are eternal investments.

When we disciple our children, cherish our spouses, and model godly character, we are building something that will last far beyond our earthly lives. These are the *"people"* who, transformed by God's grace and our faithfulness, will be part of our eternal inheritance.

Furthermore, our making *"eternal investments"* extends beyond our immediate families to include our communities and the world at large. This involves using our resources, our time, our talents, and our treasures, to advance God's purposes. It means serving the poor, advocating for justice, sharing the Gospel, and living lives that reflect Christ's love and truth.

"Your time, your love, your attention, your prayers", these are the currencies of eternal investment. Time, a non-renewable resource, becomes eternally valuable when dedicated to godly pursuits. Love, expressed sacrificially and unconditionally, builds relationships that transcend earthly boundaries.

Attention, focused on the needs and well-being of others, reflects the heart of God. And prayer, our direct communication with the Almighty, is perhaps the most potent and enduring investment of all, shaping spiritual realities and drawing heaven to earth.

Ultimately, Jesus's words in Matthew 6 are a profound challenge to examine our lives. Are we living for the fleeting comforts of this world, or are we actively laying up our treasures in heaven? Are we building on sand or on the solid rock of eternal truth? The call is clear: invest in what truly lasts, for where your treasure is, there your heart will be also.

Your kids won't remember your watch collection. They'll remember whether you looked up from your phone when they walked in. They'll remember if you showed up. They'll remember whether you treated their mom with respect. And they'll especially remember if you modeled Christ or just talked about Him on Sundays.

So, aim long. Think beyond your funeral. What do you want your great grandkids to know about you? What stories do you want retold at your table in heaven?

Walk in integrity.

> "BETTER IS A POOR MAN WHO WALKS IN HIS INTEGRITY THAN A RICH MAN WHO IS CROOKED IN HIS WAYS."
> *PROVERBS 28:6*

Legacy isn't about assets. It's about character.

Model repentance. Don't fake perfection. Own your junk. Say, "*I was wrong, will you forgive me?*" Do it in front of your kids. Let them see grace in motion.

Saturate your home in Scripture. Let God's Word be normal language, not foreign vocabulary. Let verses be on your walls, your lips, your routines.

Serve together. Don't just attend church, be the Church. Deliver meals. Help neighbors. Support missionaries. Let your kids see you bleed kingdom.

Joshua didn't whisper a private conviction. He declared for the whole tribe to hear:

"AS FOR ME AND MY HOUSE, WE WILL SERVE THE LORD"
JOSHUA 24:15.

That wasn't a suggestion. It was a family manifesto.

When the Story Is Broken

Now maybe your father was MIA. Maybe he was harsh, drunk, distracted, or worse. Maybe your inheritance is baggage. Good. Because the gospel isn't just a redemption story. It's a restart button. Second Corinthians 5:17 shouts it: "If anyone is in Christ, he is a new creation. The old has passed away, behold, the new has come."

You may not have been handed a legacy worth keeping. But you can build one worth passing on.

When a Tennessee man died unexpectedly at the age of 52 in 2023. His name wasn't well known beyond his small community. He didn't have a platform, a massive following, or a list of career accolades. He never made headlines during his life, but at his funeral, something remarkable unfolded.

Five grown children stood one by one to speak. As they approached the microphone, there was no talk of inheritance, career milestones, or worldly success. Each child shared stories that painted a vivid portrait of a man whose quiet faith had left an eternal mark. They spoke through tears, not because of unresolved wounds, but because they were mourning a man who had loved them well.

His oldest daughter, now a teacher and mother of three, remembered how every school morning began with a prayer at the breakfast table. "He laid hands on our heads and asked God to protect us, guide us, and grow our hearts to love Him," she said. "*Even when we were late, even when we rolled our eyes, he never skipped it. That consistency taught me that God was not just for Sundays.*"

His son shared how his father had prayed with him the night before every big game, not for victory, but for character. "*He prayed I'd show integrity on the field and humility in the win or loss. He said, 'Your identity isn't in your stats, son. It's in Christ.' At the time, I didn't get it. Now I do.*"

Another daughter told of how her father wrote handwritten notes and left them in her car when she started driving. They were short, simple reminders: "*You are loved. Stay close to Jesus. I'm proud of you.*"

The youngest son, now in college, remembered how his dad would sit on the edge of his bed after hard days and just listen. "*He didn't always have advice. He didn't try to fix me. He just made sure I knew I wasn't alone.*"

One of the most poignant moments came when the third child shared a rebellious season from her teenage years. "*I walked away from church. I rolled my eyes at everything he said. I slammed doors. But he never slammed one back. He never raised his voice. He just kept praying, kept reminding me that God wasn't done with me. When I hit rock bottom, he was the one waiting with open arms.*"

Friends from the community added their voices too. A neighbor said he noticed how the man always had time for his kids, whether tossing a ball in the yard, cheering at recitals, or helping with homework. "*He made fatherhood look sacred,*" the neighbor said.

A deacon from his church shared how the man led a men's Bible study for years. "*He wasn't flashy, but he was faithful. He showed up with coffee, his worn-out Bible, and a heart ready to pour into younger men.*"

This man may never be remembered by the world, but in his home and community, his influence was monumental. He built his life around the gospel, not a resume. He pursued the hearts of his children, not just their behavior. He left behind no monuments, but a legacy that will ripple through generations.

That's what it means to live rooted in Christ. That's what legacy really looks like: fierce love, constant prayer, and a life that quietly points others to Jesus.

Men, the pen is in your hand. You're writing a story. One day, your kids will read it aloud. Make it worthy. Let them say, *"My dad followed Christ, and because of him, so do I."*

Don't delay. Legacy is not a finish line. It's every step, every choice, every sacrifice.

And when your time is up, may your legacy not just be remembered, but replicated.

May they not just say you were a good man, but that you left them a path that led straight to Christ.

A Grandfathers Gift

Samuel was not a wealthy man, nor did he hold any great position in the world. He worked as a mechanic in a small town; his hands always stained with oil and his clothes smelling of grease. Yet, every morning before the sun rose, he would kneel beside his worn armchair with a Bible open on the cushion. His prayer list, scribbled on yellowing pages, grew longer as the years passed, children, grandchildren, and eventually great-grandchildren.

Decades went by, and Samuel never stopped. He prayed when his son rebelled and walked away from the church. He prayed when his daughter's marriage nearly collapsed. He prayed through sicknesses, job losses, and seasons when it seemed his family had no interest in God at all. Sometimes he wondered if his prayers were hitting the ceiling, but he kept going, whispering their names in faith.

One Christmas, when Samuel was in his eighties, the family gathered in his living room. As they ate and laughed, Samuel quietly noticed changes. His once wayward son now prayed over the meal. His daughter and her husband, once on the brink of divorce, held hands tightly. A teenage grandson leaned over and asked Samuel about his Bible, curious to learn more. Samuel's heart swelled.

When he passed away a few years later, his family found his prayer journals stacked in a box. Page after page carried their names, written faithfully year after year. As they read, tears fell. They realized the quiet power that had been covering them all along.

Samuel had never preached a sermon, never written a book, never led a movement. But his decades of prayer shaped generations. His legacy was not in accomplishments but in intercession, proving that the most influential work a man can do for his family is to faithfully carry them before the throne of God.

Reflection

- Identify the values your children would say define your life today.

- Commit to one intentional step this week in discipling the next generation.

- Examine the daily habits that are quietly shaping the fabric of your legacy.

- Confess any patterns that may be weakening your legacy and seek God's help to rebuild them.

Prayer

Lord, teach me to number my days and live with eternity in view. Shape my habits into seeds that bear lasting fruit. Forgive where I've failed and rebuild what is broken. Let my legacy point my children and others to Your truth, Your grace, and Your glory. In Jesus' name, Amen.

Money, Work, Eternity

"Whatever you do, work heartily, as for the Lord and not for men..." Colossians 3:23

In a culture that equates a man's value with his bank balance, job title, or square footage, Scripture offers a radically different vision. Work and money are not denied in the biblical story, but they are redefined. They are not gods to be served, but tools to be stewarded, hammers in the hand of a builder, instruments for provision, discipleship, worship, and impact.

Success is not measured by accumulation. It is measured by stewardship. A man of God sees his paycheck as an offering, his work as worship, and his possessions as tools for service. His worth is not in his portfolio but in his pursuit of righteousness, his devotion to his family, and his obedience to Christ.

Redeeming Work Under Christ

Work is not a curse. Before the fall Adam was placed in the garden *"to work it and keep it"*. Only after sin entered did work become painful toil. That distinction matters. It means work is not the enemy. Your job, your trade, your calling is not a distraction from spiritual life, it is spiritual life.

But sin distorts. It turns ambition into idolatry and vocation into vanity. Jesus did not mince words:

"YOU CANNOT SERVE GOD AND MONEY"
MATTHEW 6:24

116

Many men try. They bow at the altar of hustle, convinced that overtime equals honor and that stress is a badge of success. But the Bible slams the brakes on that kind of thinking. Psalm 24:1 reminds us that everything we have, including our next breath, belongs to God. You are not the owner; you are the steward.

Work as Worship: Sacred in the Ordinary

God unequivocally calls men to a life of diligent labor, but this calling is distinct from finding their intrinsic worth or identity in the fruits of their efforts.

This verse transcends mere occupational duties, extending to every facet of a man's life. No task is too menial to carry eternal weight.

"WHATEVER YOUR HAND FINDS TO DO, DO IT WITH YOUR MIGHT."
ECCLESIASTES 9:10

The Kingdom does not rank tasks by status or salary. Faithfulness is the great equalizer.

God is not impressed by the corner office, nor dismissive of the workshop. What matters is the heart behind the hands, the motive, the worship, the surrender. A man who swings a hammer with humility and prayer may well be building more for eternity than the one who signs million-dollar contracts with selfish ambition.

Stories from the Field

Take the example of Jordan Montgomery, a Christian HVAC technician from Kentucky. For years, he wrestled with the quiet frustration that his work wasn't *"spiritual enough."* Fixing air conditioners felt far removed from ministry, and he often wondered if his life genuinely counted for the kingdom.

But as his faith deepened, Jordan began to see his work differently. Suddenly, each service call became more than a transaction. Before walking into a home, he would pause to pray, asking God to help him serve with excellence, honesty, and integrity.

Over time, something remarkable happened. His consistent kindness and trustworthy workmanship earned him a reputation that spoke louder than words. Families began to ask questions, and opportunities for gospel conversations opened up in living rooms where church invitations would have been declined.

For Jordan, tightening a bolt or replacing a coil was no longer just about restoring comfort. It became a way of bearing witness, a living testimony that faithfulness in ordinary work carries eternal weight.

Contrast that with Daniel Li, a believer working in corporate finance in New York City. Surrounded by high stakes, ruthless competition, and relentless ambition, he once found himself tempted to cut corners for career advancement.

But remembering his call to be salt and light, he chose integrity instead, even when it meant losing a deal. That decision sparked curiosity among his colleagues, leading to open conversations about why he prioritizes faith over profit. For Daniel, spreadsheets and negotiations have become his mission field, where integrity and faithfulness shine brightly.

And then there's Jeff, a stay-at-home dad in Texas, who wrestled for years with feeling *"less than"* because he wasn't the breadwinner. Yet as he leaned into God's design, he began to see that discipling his children, packing lunches, and leading morning devotions were not small tasks but kingdom-sized assignments. His living room became a training ground for future disciples, and his children now carry the marks of his faithful, unseen ministry.

These stories remind us that legacy and impact are not reserved for pulpits or platforms. They are forged in ordinary faithfulness. The question is never *how visible* your work is, but *who are you working for.*

This is precisely what Paul captures:

"SO, WHETHER YOU EAT OR DRINK, OR WHATEVER YOU DO, DO ALL TO THE GLORY OF GOD."
1 CORINTHIANS 10:31

The power of that verse lies in its inclusiveness, *whatever you do.* It demolishes the false hierarchy that places preaching above plumbing or parenting below professional success. Instead, it declares that when done unto the Lord, every task becomes sacred, every responsibility becomes worship, and every vocation becomes ministry.

When a man embraces this truth, he is liberated from the exhausting treadmill of proving his worth through worldly accolades. He now doesn't need to chase affirmation in boardrooms, applause on stages, or recognition in bank accounts.

His identity is anchored not in what he achieves, but in whose he is. This shift transforms the daily grind into a daily offering. It turns work from a burden into a blessing, and provision from mere survival into discipleship in action.

God wastes nothing. No task is too small. No worker is unseen. The plumber, the executive, and the father each display the father's heart when they serve with integrity and love. Their value does not rest in money or status. It rests in faithfulness to Christ, who dignifies their labor forever.

From Shepherds to Carpenters

The Bible itself is filled with men who's so-called *"ordinary work"* became holy ground.

Moses shepherded in Midian before leading Israel.

David tended sheep before tending a nation.

Amos dressed sycamore figs before preaching God's fire.

Paul made tents to fund his ministry.

And Jesus Himself spent most of His earthly life as a carpenter in Nazareth.

God does not divide life into sacred and secular. He weaves calling and craft together. Shepherds' fields, workshops, and job sites become altars when men labor in obedience.

These examples underscore a profound theological truth: God uses workplaces as mission fields and Monday morning meetings as discipleship labs. The so-called *"secular"* world is not a sphere outside of God's redemptive purposes; it is a primary arena for His work.

The cubicle, the construction site, the classroom, and the kitchen table are all altars where worship takes place.

For the godly man, husband, and father, this understanding changes everything. The mundane becomes sacred. The ordinary becomes worship.

His daily occupation, whether leading a team, repairing a pipe, serving a meal, or balancing a budget, is no longer just about survival or success. It becomes an extension of his devotion to God, an opportunity to embody the character of Christ in the everyday.

The way he works reveals the way he believes. In the office, on the factory floor, or in the service industry, every task carries spiritual weight.

He demonstrates integrity when shortcuts tempt. He pursues excellence when apathy beckons. He serves with humility when selfish ambition lurks.

In this way, his work itself becomes testimony, a living sermon to those around him, declaring that Christ is Lord over every square inch of life.

In doing so, he shines as a light in a dark world. Not primarily through eloquent words, but through faithful presence, humble service, and uncompromising integrity.

His coworkers and clients may never set foot inside a church building, yet they encounter the fragrance of Christ in how he handles stress, honors people, and carries himself with joy and peace. For him, work is no longer just about making a living. It becomes a living testimony to the God who redeems every moment.

Moreover, the workplace itself becomes a vital setting for discipleship. It is the arena where faith is either proven genuine or exposed as hollow. Every office, job site, and shop floor carries countless opportunities. A chance to mentor colleagues, to embody biblical principles under pressure, and to cultivate a culture of respect and godliness.

Paul reminds us,

> "DO ALL THINGS WITHOUT GRUMBLING OR DISPUTING, THAT YOU MAY BE BLAMELESS AND INNOCENT, CHILDREN OF GOD WITHOUT BLEMISH IN THE MIDST OF A CROOKED AND TWISTED GENERATION, AMONG WHOM YOU SHINE AS LIGHTS IN THE WORLD."
> *PHILIPPIANS 2:14–15*

Seen in this light, difficult clients, demanding deadlines, and strained relationships are no longer just inconveniences. They are sanctifying assignments, designed for growth, and opportunities to demonstrate reliance on God.

The godly man sees his professional sphere as a classroom where he learns patience, perseverance, humility, and prayer, and where he has the privilege of influencing others for Christ. His vocational calling is no longer about climbing ladders or padding resumes. It is about living out his faith vibrantly and intentionally, becoming a flesh-and-blood testimony of God's transforming power woven into the very fabric of society. His paycheck sustains his household, but his presence at work advances the kingdom.

When you view your work through the lens of Scripture, the pressure to prove yourself fades. You don't need to out-earn your peers to be faithful. You don't need to climb the ladder to make a kingdom impact. You just need to show up, work with integrity, and remember who your real boss is.

The Danger of Money as Master

Your paycheck is a tool to bless others, not just to accumulate stuff. Proverbs 3:9 calls us to *"Honor the Lord with your wealth and with the first fruits of all your produce."* That means generosity isn't optional, it's fundamental. Tithing, supporting missionaries, helping a brother in need, these are acts of war against the idol of greed.

The real legacy of a man isn't measured by his bank account, but by his obedience. Are you using your work to reflect Christ? Are you discipling younger men in your trade? Are you pointing your coworkers toward something eternal?

The world says success is a corner office. God says success is faithfulness in whatever corner you're assigned.

You are not what you make. You are who God says you are. And He says you're His workmanship, created in Christ Jesus for good works. That includes your job.

So, show up. Clock in. Work hard. Give thanks. And do it all in the name of the Lord Jesus Christ.

The goal is not to eliminate ambition. The world has enough passive, visionless men. Godly ambition is a fire that needs direction, not extinction. Work should be fueled by mission, not ego. It is no longer about carving your name in stone, but about writing His name on hearts.

Whether you lay bricks, run spreadsheets, close deals, or teach middle schoolers, your job is not just a paycheck, it is a platform. It is where your integrity gets tested and your faith gets legs. When you offer your labor to God, the mundane becomes sacred.

You do not need a church stage to preach the gospel. You do it when you refuse to gossip at the job site, when you show patience with a difficult client, when you give credit to a junior teammate. The excellence of your work and the character behind it speak volumes. Your job can either echo with eternity or die with the paycheck.

Too many men live in a split reality, treating Sunday morning as God's domain and Monday morning as their own. But Christ lays claim to all of it. There is no sacred–secular divide in the kingdom of God. Every hour, every task, every interaction is an opportunity to glorify Him.

When you serve others with integrity, you are doing holy work.

When you show up early, finish well, pray before meetings, and thank God after victories, your labor becomes worship. It is no longer just about earning a paycheck. It is about shaping a testimony.

Your coworkers, employees, and clients see it. More importantly, your children see it. They learn that God is present in the ordinary, that faith is not confined to a pew, but lived out in the grit of daily labor.

In a world where mediocrity is normal and compromise is expected, excellence is evangelism. It makes people ask questions. It opens doors. It sets you apart. And when they ask why you're different, you don't point to your work ethic, you point to your Savior.

"IF ANYONE DOES NOT PROVIDE FOR HIS RELATIVES, AND ESPECIALLY FOR MEMBERS OF HIS HOUSEHOLD, HE HAS DENIED THE FAITH."
1 TIMOTHY 5:8

That is strong language. But it's not just about groceries and rent. Provision means spiritual leadership, emotional presence, and moral clarity.

Provide a spiritual foundation by reading the Word with your family. Provide emotional security by being a safe place of encouragement. Provide wisdom by modeling repentance and accountability. Your provision is not just a salary; it is a channel for God's grace.

In recent years, billionaires have stepped away from their thrones. Jack Dorsey left Twitter. Jeff Bezos stepped down from Amazon. Many cited burnout and relational ruin. One tech founder famously said, "*I won the rat race, but I was still a rat.*" These men hit the top and found it hollow.

Dan Price, the CEO who raised his employees' minimum salary to $70,000 by slashing his own, made headlines not for making more, but for giving more. Though his personal life later spiraled, the move itself forced a conversation: What if success is about blessing others, not bloating your ego?

Paul, in his letter to Timothy, delivers a stark warning:

"For the love of money is a root of all kinds of evils"
1 Timothy 6:10.

Notice that Paul does not condemn money itself. Money is not evil by nature. It is a tool. It meets needs, allows exchange, and can fuel generosity and kingdom work. The danger lies in its seduction.

Money whispers promise. It promises security in a world that feels fragile. It promises power, the ability to shape life to our desires. It promises freedom, convincing us we can escape limits. It promises comfort, drawing us with indulgence.

These promises are hollow. When money takes the place of master, it corrupts. It twists values. It feeds greed. It demands compromise. Jesus said it plainly:

"YOU CANNOT SERVE BOTH GOD AND MONEY"
MATTHEW 6:24

The results are tragic. Families fracture under the weight of endless career pursuits. Marriages bend under financial stress. Friendships snap for the sake of gain. Hearts grow dull to the presence of God. Money, when worshiped, will always betray.

But when money is surrendered to Christ, it becomes holy. It provides, it blesses, it fuels generosity and mission. In His hands, it builds rather than destroys.

Weapons Against Greed

A godly man fights money's pull with three weapons: Contentment, Simplicity, and Generosity.

When a man fights with these weapons, he does more than resist greed; he builds a legacy. His family learns to see possessions as tools, not idols. His children inherit not just financial provision but a pattern of faith, gratitude, and open-handed living that echoes into eternity.

Is your 401(k) bigger than your Kingdom investment? Are you discipling your kids or just buying them stuff? Does your money reflect your mission?

Faithfulness, not fortune, is God's metric. The widow who gave two coins was praised above all the donors. She did not have much, but she gave it all. Jesus said,

> *"WELL DONE, GOOD AND FAITHFUL SERVANT,"*
> MATTHEW 25:23

Notice he didn't say my successful servant? The word proclaims,

> *"THE EARTH IS THE LORD'S AND THE FULLNESS THEREOF."*
> PSALM 24:1

That includes your wallet. That includes your work schedule. You are a steward. Stewards budget wisely (Proverbs 21:5), avoid debt (Proverbs 22:7), save diligently (Proverbs 6:6–8), and give joyfully (Mark 12:44).

Stewardship kills entitlement. It turns spending into worship. It reframes money from "*mine*" to "*His.*" Every dollar becomes a decision about Kingdom or comfort.

Training the Next Generation

Proverbs 22:6 commands fathers to train their children. That training includes work ethics and financial wisdom. If you do not disciple your kids in these areas, TikTok and YouTube gladly will.

- Teach them the dignity of work.

- Show them how to budget.

- Let them watch you tithe with joy.

- Invite them into generosity.

Because when you do, everything changes. Your job becomes worship. Your money becomes mission. And your legacy becomes eternal.

Let the world chase status. Let you chase Christ.

And when your time is up, may they not just say you worked hard, but that you worked holy. Let every dollar, every task, every hour be stamped with the glory of God.

That, brothers, is biblical manhood in action.

Not Failing

Jonathan was a man everyone admired from a distance. He worked tirelessly, built a successful business, and provided his family with every comfort they could ask for. The house was large, the cars were new, and vacations were frequent. He told himself that all the long nights and missed dinners were for them, that one day his wife and children would thank him for the sacrifices he made.

But slowly, cracks appeared. His wife, Sarah, grew weary of raising the children largely on her own. His daughter stopped asking him to come to her soccer games because she knew he would be too busy. His son, once eager to share stories from school, learned to keep them to himself. Jonathan's absence was not marked by malice but by misplaced love, he gave them things but withheld himself.

One evening, he came home late to find Sarah waiting at the kitchen table, tears in her eyes. She told him plainly, "We don't need more from your business, we need more from you." The words stung, but

Jonathan brushed them aside, promising that the season of busyness would soon pass. It never did.

Years later, Jonathan sat in that same kitchen, this time in silence. His children were grown, living their own lives, and their distance from him was more than geographical. They had built walls where bridges should have been. He had succeeded in his career but failed in his first calling as a husband and father.

Jonathan's story is a warning. Success in the world cannot replace presence at home. A man can win in the marketplace and lose the very hearts he was called to shepherd. True legacy is not found in possessions but in relationships, in the unseen moments of love, prayer, and sacrifice that no paycheck can buy.

Work holy. Give generously. Live faithfully. That, brothers, is biblical manhood in action.

Reflection

- Identify where you've been treating work as mere survival or status instead of worship.

- Confess ways you've rooted your identity in success, income, or position rather than Christ.

- Evaluate how your financial decisions reflect pursuit of comfort versus stewardship for God's glory.

- Commit to modeling financial faithfulness, through contentment, simplicity, and generosity, within your home.

Prayer

Lord, thank You for the gift of work and the resources You entrust to me. Guard my heart from greed and the love of money. Teach me contentment in Your presence, simplicity in my living, and joy in generosity. Let my labor honor You, my stewardship reflect Christ, and my legacy point my family to eternal treasure. In Jesus' name, Amen.

Trials, Temptations, Testing

"Count it all joy, my brothers, when you meet trials of various kinds, for you know that the testing of your faith produces steadfastness." James 1:2–3

Every man will face fire. Not only the external pressures of work, family, and responsibility, but also the internal furnace where faith is refined, motives are laid bare, and character is forged. Scripture does not hide this reality; it prepares us for it.

"THE LORD TESTS THE RIGHTEOUS"
PSALM 11:5

If you belong to God, you will face the fire. Yet His testing is never meant to destroy you, but to purify, strengthen, and equip you for greater faithfulness.

From Genesis to Revelation, God's story is filled with men who walked through fire. Abraham was tested with the unthinkable call to offer his son. Joseph was betrayed by his brothers, falsely accused, and unjustly imprisoned.

David, though anointed as king, fled for his life and hid in caves, waiting for years for the promise to be fulfilled. And even Jesus, the very Son of God, was tested in the wilderness.

Refining Fires, Not Random Misfortunes

And today, the fire still burns. For one man it is the sudden layoff that shatters financial security. For another, it's the cancer diagnosis that rewrites his family's future. For some, it's betrayal by a close friend, or the slow grind of unanswered prayers.

These are not random misfortunes, they are refining fires. They strip away false idols, expose flimsy foundations, and draw us to the only Rock that cannot be shaken.

The testing of your faith is not a side road or an interruption; it is the very path God uses to mature you into a man who can bear the weight of His calling.

"WE REJOICE IN OUR SUFFERINGS, KNOWING THAT SUFFERING PRODUCES ENDURANCE, AND ENDURANCE PRODUCES CHARACTER, AND CHARACTER PRODUCES HOPE."
ROMANS 5:3–4

God never wastes our pain. Trials expose the things we've trusted in besides Christ. They refine our affections. They draw us back to dependency. They reveal what really sustains us.

In 2023, during a national economic crisis, countless men faced layoffs, health scares, and family breakdowns. Yet many testified that their faith had never been stronger. Why? Because when every earthly support was stripped away, Christ became their anchor. Trials teach us that God is not just enough, He is everything.

James instructs,

"COUNT IT ALL JOY, MY BROTHERS, WHEN YOU MEET TRIALS OF VARIOUS KINDS, FOR YOU KNOW THAT THE TESTING OF YOUR FAITH PRODUCES STEADFASTNESS."
JAMES 1:2–4

Trials are not random; they are customized tools in the hands of a loving Father. They produce depth where there was shallowness, wisdom where there was presumption, and resilience where there was fragility.

The Counterfeit Fire

If trials refine, temptation seeks to consume. James 1:14 shows us temptation springs from within, while 1 Corinthians 10:13 promises it is resistible through God's faithfulness.

Dietrich Bonhoeffer warned, *"Sin demands to have a man by himself."* Isolation makes us vulnerable; honest community fortifies us.

John divides temptation into three categories, the same three Jesus faced in the wilderness: the lust of the flesh, the lust of the eyes, and the pride of life. These mirror the temptations Jesus faced in the wilderness, and they are still the primary weapons Satan uses today.

- **Lust of the Flesh** - Misuse of physical desires. In our porn-saturated culture, this is war. Purity is not just absence of sin, but the presence of holiness, accountability, guardrails, and retrained affections.

- **Lust of the Eyes** - Craving possessions, status, and wealth. Social media fuels comparison, but Jesus warned, *"One's life does not consist in the abundance of possessions"*.

- **Pride of Life** - The socially acceptable sin of self-glorification. It's independence without God.

The antidote? The presence of Christ. Like Jesus, we fight temptation not with willpower but with worship, declaring *"It is written."*

This is not a side struggle; it is war. Pornography is not a private habit, it is a spiritual assault on your soul, your marriage, and your witness.

Barna reports that 54% of practicing Christian's view pornography occasionally; about 22% do so weekly or daily. (Barna, Beyond the Porn Phenomenon, 2024) The lie is subtle but lethal: *"It doesn't hurt anyone. Everyone does it.*" But sin doesn't need to shout to destroy. It whispers. It isolates. It corrodes the heart in silence.

The battle for purity is not about shame, it is about freedom. It is about refusing to surrender your mind and body to the enemy and choosing instead to present them as living sacrifices, holy and acceptable to God.

In 2021, a Christian NFL player spoke publicly about his battle with sexual addiction and how accountability through a men's Bible study and daily Scripture intake helped break years of bondage. He stated, "*It wasn't just about avoiding sin. It was about learning to worship God with my body.*"

Lust of the Eyes is the craving for possessions, status, and wealth. We are tempted to compare, to covet, and to chase after worldly success.

"THE EYES OF MAN ARE NEVER SATISFIED."
PROVERBS 27:20

Contentment is not the result of having more, but of treasuring Christ above all.

Social media pours gasoline on this temptation. Instagram influences flaunt wealth, bodies, and lifestyles that whisper, "*You're not enough.*" Men start to measure their worth not by the fruit of the Spirit but by square footage, follower counts, and car models. But Jesus flips that script. He says,

"TAKE CARE, AND BE ON YOUR GUARD AGAINST ALL COVETOUSNESS,
FOR ONE'S LIFE DOES NOT CONSIST IN THE ABUNDANCE OF HIS
POSSESSIONS."
LUKE 12:15

In 2023, a well-known Silicon Valley executive sold his multimillion-dollar company and donated half his wealth to missions in unreached countries. When asked why, he simply said, "*I was tired of being full of stuff but empty of joy.*"

Pride of Life is the subtle sin of self-glorification. It's the belief that we can succeed apart from God. It manifests as prayerlessness, arrogance, and a refusal to ask for help.

This is perhaps the most socially acceptable sin in the church. We idolize independence, platform, and influence. We applaud confidence, often mistaking it for conviction. Yet Scripture is clear: God doesn't share His glory. Pride is what turned Lucifer into Satan. It's what drove Pharaoh to destruction. And it's what will bring down any man who forgets his need for God.

Practical Weapons for the Battle

Victory is possible, but only with the right weapons:

- Meditate on Scripture daily.
- Confess regularly in trusted community.
- Pray without ceasing.
- Avoid triggers and flee temptation.

The antidote to these three poisons is the presence of Christ. Jesus faced all three in the wilderness and overcame them with the Word. We don't fight with willpower; we fight with worship. We don't conquer by effort alone, but by abiding in the One who already overcame.

Guard your heart, brother. Fix your eyes on Jesus. Reject the lies that promise life and deliver death. Run the race with endurance. And know that every temptation resisted is one more stake driven into the ground of your spiritual legacy.

Jesus resisted by declaring, "It is written." The Word of God is the weapon He gives us. A Bible in our hands is not the goal. God's truth must live in our hearts.

James 4:7 gives us the formula: *"Submit yourselves therefore to God. Resist the devil, and he will flee from you."* Victory in temptation is not about willpower, but surrender.

It begins with submitting to God, yielding your will, your desires, and your thought life. Then, with the armor of God, you resist.

Endurance: The Long Road of Faith

In 2024, a men's ministry in Texas saw dramatic breakthrough among men battling sexual addiction by implementing three disciplines: a weekly confession, Scripture memory, and daily prayer partners. God honors intentionality.

Failure is not the end of your story. Peter denied Christ three times, yet Jesus restored him and commissioned him to shepherd His people. The prodigal son squandered his inheritance, but the father ran to embrace him with open arms.

Righteous men fall, not once, but repeatedly. What makes them righteous is not their perfection but their perseverance. God does not define you by your worst moment. He defines you by Christ's finished work.

If you've fallen:

- Repent honestly before God.
- Seek forgiveness from those you've hurt.
- Rebuild spiritual rhythms.
- Reconnect with community.

Your story can become a testimony. Your weakness can become a witness. God redeems what the enemy tried to destroy.

Life will not get easier. The storms will not lessen. But your roots can grow deeper.

Jesus said in Matthew 7:24–25 that the wise man builds his house on the rock. When, not if, the storm comes, it stands firm. Build your life on Christ. Invest in spiritual disciplines. Cultivate friendships with other godly men. Guard your heart.

"RUN WITH ENDURANCE THE RACE THAT IS SET BEFORE US, LOOKING
TO JESUS, THE FOUNDER AND PERFECTER OF OUR FAITH."
HEBREWS 12:1–2

The race is long. The trials are real. But Christ is the prize, and He runs with you.

Tested, Tried, and True

Brother, testing is not punishment. It is preparation. God is not trying to break you; He is building you. Every fire is refining your faith. Every trial is training your character. Every temptation resisted is strengthening your spirit.

Consider Job, who endured loss, grief, sickness, and isolation. He lost his children, his wealth, and even the support of his wife, who told him to curse God and die. His friends accused him of hidden sin. But Job clung to God.

"BUT HE KNOWS THE WAY THAT I TAKE; WHEN HE HAS TRIED ME, I
SHALL COME OUT AS GOLD."
JOB 23:10

That kind of faith is forged, not found. It is shaped in the furnace of affliction, not in comfort.

In more recent times, we can look to the story of Horatio Spafford. In the late 1800s, Spafford lost his son to illness, his fortune in the Great Chicago Fire, and then all four of his daughters in a shipwreck.

As he sailed across the Atlantic to join his grieving wife, he penned the famous hymn "*It Is Well with My Soul.*" This was not the product of a peaceful life but of a tested and anchored faith. His words have brought hope to millions because they were born in the crucible of sorrow.

Endurance looks different for every man. For some, it means staying faithful in a job that feels thankless but provides for the family. For others, it is waking up every day to care for a special-needs child with relentless love. For others still, it is resisting the call of old addictions and choosing accountability and sobriety.

Endurance is not loud. It doesn't post on social media or seek applause. It quietly shows up. It worships when feelings are gone. It prays when answers are delayed. It serves when gratitude is absent. It forgives when bitterness feels easier. It stands firm when compromise is more convenient.

The great preacher Charles Spurgeon once said, "*By perseverance the snail reached the ark.*" That's a man who understood grit. Endurance is not about flash; it's about faithfulness.

And here's the truth: you do not endure alone. Christ is with you. He endured the cross, despising its shame, and now He intercedes for you at the right hand of the Father. He is not distant from your suffering. He was tempted in every way, yet without sin. He knows your pain. He hears your cry. He bottles your tears.

You may feel like you are walking through fire, but so did the three Hebrew boys in Daniel 3. Shadrach, Meshach, and Abednego were thrown into a furnace for refusing to bow to a false god. But when the

137

king looked in, he saw a fourth man walking with them, "*like a son of the gods*". They were not alone in the flames. Neither are you.

Maybe today your trial is a crumbling marriage. Or a prodigal child. Or a deep anxiety you can't shake. Perhaps it's a financial crisis or a health diagnosis. Whatever the furnace, the fire is not the end. It is the proving ground of your faith.

Scripture never promises comfort. But it promises Christ. He is enough. And His grace is sufficient.

So, stand firm. Hold fast. Rise again.

You may limp across the finish line. You may be bruised, bleeding, and breathless. But Christ will be there, arms wide, saying, "*Well done.*"

Faithfulness in the Small Things

Greatness is measured in the prayers whispered in the dark, the dishes washed in love, the integrity maintained at work, and the tender presence at the bedside of a child. This is the kind of greatness that doesn't trend on social media but reverberates in eternity.

"MOREOVER, IT IS REQUIRED OF STEWARDS THAT THEY BE FOUND
FAITHFUL"
1 CORINTHIANS 4:2.

In the economy of heaven, faithfulness is the currency of greatness.

God doesn't reward the most famous or the most followed. He rewards those who are faithful with what they've been given, whether the assignment looks big or small in the eyes of the world.

Being a godly man isn't about heroic sprints of holiness; it's about the long, steady marathon of ordinary obedience. And let's be honest: it's a lot easier to run 100 yards with everyone clapping than it is to walk 10,000 unseen steps each day when no one is watching.

The Christian life is often lived out not in front of an audience, but in obscurity. Changing diapers. Showing up to work. Checking the oil in your wife's car. Picking up groceries. Listening attentively when you're exhausted. Doing the dishes even when you have already cooked dinner.

These are not second-tier spiritual activities. They are the very battlefield where character is forged.

Remember, Jesus spent 30 of His 33 years on earth in relative obscurity, working as a carpenter in a dusty village no one cared about. If mundane faithfulness was worthy of the Son of God, it is certainly worthy of us.

How you handle the trash can reflect how you'll handle a title. If we cannot be faithful in the small, how can we be trusted with the large? Great character is not built in the spotlight; it's built in secret. Obedience in obscurity is what prepares a man for influence.

Faithfulness in Marriage

A faithful husband is not simply one who avoids adultery. That's the bare minimum.

Faithfulness in marriage is marked by a steady consistency, love, service, and presence woven into daily life. It's heard in kind words at the end of a long day. It's seen in how he speaks about his wife when she's not in the room. It's felt when he chooses her well-being over his own convenience.

Faithfulness shows up in the quiet, unseen moments: praying for her without needing for her to know. It's making the bed though he was the last one up, listening to her dreams and fears as if they matter, because they do.

Faithfulness is found in choosing gentleness when frustration rises, in choosing to say "*I love you*" when routine tries to replace romance, and in staying emotionally engaged even when distractions abound. Faithfulness in marriage is often not dramatic. It's the thousand small decisions to keep your covenant, to lean in rather than drift away, to hold fast when the world says let go.

Faithfulness in Fatherhood

Your children are not looking for perfection. They are desperate for presence. A father who shows up consistently, through bedtime prayers, school drop-offs, Saturday morning pancakes, and apologies when he loses his temper, is a mighty force in shaping identity.

In numerous studies, researchers discovered a simple but profound truth: it's not the quantity of time that anchors a child's heart, but the consistency of positive interactions. (Lippold MA, 2015) In other words, your kid doesn't need a superhero. They need a steady, safe, present man.

It's not about fireworks and grand gestures. It's about showing up, repeatedly. The bedtime story. The listening ear. The calm presence when life feels chaotic. These are the rhythms that build security and trust, the quiet bricks of fatherhood that create an unshakable foundation.

When a father apologizes, he teaches humility. When he shows up, game after game, mistake after mistake, he communicates, *"You matter."* When he puts down his phone and looks his child in the eye, he is silently declaring, *"I'm here."*

Faithfulness in fatherhood is your superpower. It doesn't trend, it doesn't go viral, but it builds an invisible foundation strong enough for your children to stand on.

Faithfulness at Work

Labor is not merely a means to a paycheck; it is a field of discipleship. That means when you pray quietly before a meeting, when you refuse to cut corners on a jobsite, when you answer calmly instead of with anger at a difficult customer, you are preaching a sermon no pulpit ever could.

Your children see it too. They notice when Dad works with integrity, when he comes home tired but still chooses patience, when he thanks God for the paycheck instead of complaining about the grind.

Faithfulness in the office, on the factory floor, or behind the wheel of a truck echoes the same message you send from the bleachers: *"I'm here. I'm steady. And I belong to Christ."*

God sees your integrity when no one else does. He sees your diligence when the promotion passes you by. He notices how you treat coworkers, how you respond under pressure, and how you steward even small measures of influence. Faithfulness in the workplace is never wasted, it builds your character, shapes your reputation, and often opens unseen doors for ministry.

Consider Nehemiah. Before he ever rebuilt Jerusalem's walls, he was a cupbearer to the king, a role of quiet faithfulness, trust, and integrity in a foreign court. His diligence in that position earned the king's respect, opening the door for him to lead one of the most pivotal restoration projects in Israel's history. Nehemiah's example reminds us that our *"ordinary"* work is often the training ground for extraordinary assignments.

The man who pursues peace rather than conflict. The man who confesses his faults rather than hiding them. The man who works with integrity even when unseen. That is the man God can trust with more. His steady obedience may never be noticed online, but it is honored in heaven.

And even when no one applauds, heaven notices.

Faithfulness in Spiritual Disciplines

Scripture encourages us,

> "LET US NOT GROW WEARY OF DOING GOOD, FOR IN DUE SEASON WE
> WILL REAP, IF WE DO NOT GIVE UP."
> *GALATIANS 6:9*

The spiritual disciplines, prayer, Scripture reading, fasting, family devotions, church attendance, may not feel exciting, but they form the inner life of a man rooted in Christ. They are not optional religious accessories, they are lifelines.

There are mornings when the Bible feels dry, when prayer feels mechanical, when your heart feels numb. But faithfulness says, "*I will show up anyway.*" The man who returns daily to the Word, who keeps leading his family even when discouraged, who prays through the silence, he is the man God strengthens.

These practices are the hidden roots of a mighty tree. They do not grow overnight, but they grow deep, making you unshakeable when the storms hit. And make no mistake, storms will come.

Faithfulness does not mean perfection. It does not mean the absence of failure. It does not mean religious show. Faithfulness is returning to Jesus. It rises again after every fall. It is steady obedience when others turn back. It is choosing consistency over charisma, obedience over outcomes, presence over performance.

The faithful man knows he will stumble, but he also knows he is held by a faithful God. He doesn't measure his worth by success but by surrender.

Faithfulness is choosing obedience over emotion. It's shown in staying the course when others take shortcuts. It's praying again, even when last prayer felt empty.

It's keeping the promises no one else remembers. It's canceling the porn subscription, not just because you got caught, but because you love your wife. It's doing the right thing when the wrong thing would be easier and more fun.

Faithfulness in the Everyday

Andrew worked at a manufacturing plant where the pressure to meet quotas was constant. Many of his coworkers had learned to cut corners, skipping steps in safety checks, ignoring small defects, or rushing orders out the door, because the bosses only seemed to care about numbers.

But Andrew was different. He believed that every task, no matter how small, was a matter of stewardship before God. When others skipped steps, he quietly stayed late to make sure the work was done right. When a supervisor urged him to sign off on a shipment without proper inspection, Andrew respectfully refused. His coworkers mocked him, saying he cared too much about details no one noticed.

Months later, a major defect was discovered in a batch that had been rushed through by others. The company faced serious consequences. Yet when management reviewed Andrew's section, every report was clean and every product sound. His integrity had spared the company greater loss.

What stood out even more was his spirit. Andrew never gloated, never shamed his coworkers, and never demanded recognition. He simply kept working with quiet diligence. Over time, others noticed. A younger employee, once skeptical, admitted, "You have shown me what it means to take pride in my work the right way."

Andrew's story reminds us that character is not proven in grand moments but in daily choices. Cutting corners may seem to save time, but it erodes trust and excellence. Doing the right thing, even when unseen, builds a legacy of reliability that honors both God and others.

Modern Parables of Quiet Greatness

In an eye-opening memoir, a hospice nurse recorded the most common stories shared by dying men. And you know what? They were not about business achievements or trophies on the wall. They were about their dad packing lunches, hugging them through heartbreak, and whispering prayers in hospital rooms. None of them said, "*I wish Dad had closed more deals.*" They said, "*I'm so grateful he was there.*"

The things we think go unnoticed are the very things that leave an eternal imprint. Faithfulness lives in the margins, in the quiet routines, in the small acts of love, in the unwavering presence of a man who refuses to quit. When your kids are grown and your wife is gray, what they will remember is whether you were there, not whether you were impressive.

Faithfulness is not maintained by sheer willpower. It is fueled by God's unfailing love.

A janitor named James Fenn in Michigan quietly retired in 2021 after 42 years of service at the same elementary school. He was never promoted. He never earned headlines. But on his last day, the entire student body lined the halls, holding hand-written signs that read, *"Thank you, Mr. James."* Parents spoke about how he greeted every child by name and prayed over the school before the sun rose. His legacy wasn't in wealth, but in witness.

A single father in Ohio worked two jobs for over a decade to put his daughter through college. When she graduated, she wept not for the diploma, but for the faithfulness that got her there. *"My dad never missed a recital, even when it meant skipping sleep,"* she said. *"He showed me what love looks like."*

In a world obsessed with fleeting fame and digital trends, true greatness often blossoms in the quiet corners of consistent faithfulness. We live in an age where virality is king, where accomplishments are tallied in likes, shares, and headline appearances. Yet the eternal ledger of heaven records a different kind of heroism, one steeped in steadfastness, humble service, and unwavering integrity.

Consider Harold, a deacon in a small Kansas church. His ministry was far from the spotlight. For thirty-five years, rain or shine, he faithfully served in the church parking lot. There were no microphones, no grand sermons, no groundbreaking initiatives. Just a man with a servant's heart, showing up week after week.

Harold's impact was not measured in numbers but in moments: the warm smile that greeted weary families, the quiet prayer whispered with widows, the steady presence who looked out for struggling single mothers. His life, never broadcast on major platforms, was a living sermon of quiet consistency.

Heaven counts that kind of greatness. Jesus said,

"THE GREATEST AMONG YOU WILL BE YOUR SERVANT"
MATTHEW 23:11

Harold's faithfulness, hidden from the world, resounded in eternity. And it is this kind of greatness, quiet, steady, unseen, that God still calls men to today.

The ripple effect of Harold's faithfulness extended far beyond what he could ever imagine. One young man, now a pastor himself, recounted his first encounter with Harold at the age of 11. "*I came to church for the first time at age 11 and met Harold in the parking lot,*" he recalled. "*He was the first man who ever made me feel safe. That day changed my life.*"

This profound declaration speaks volumes about the immeasurable power of a life lived with intentional kindness and dependable character. Harold didn't need a massive platform; his simple act of being present and compassionate was enough to alter the trajectory of a young boy's life.

These are the narratives that rarely grace the trending lists of TikTok or find their way into the pages of Fortune magazine. The world clamors for flash and spectacle, for overnight successes and meteoric rises. But the divine perspective is profoundly different. Heaven keeps a record that values depth over superficiality, grit over glamour, and enduring commitment over fleeting popularity.

The Call to Show Up

For the godly man, faithfulness is showing up:

- **Physically** present at school plays, games, and kitchen tables.

- **Emotionally** listening, empathizing, validating, forgiving.

- **Spiritually** leading your family in prayer, Scripture, worship, and integrity.

It means sacrifice, reprioritizing, forgiving again, and living with integrity when it costs you.

The Eternal Record

Lamentations 3:22–23 reminds us: *"The steadfast love of the Lord never ceases... His mercies are new every morning."* God fuels our faithfulness with His own.

"DO NOT DESPISE SMALL BEGINNINGS."
ZECHARIAH 4:10

Celebrate small victories. Heaven records every act of obedience.

Reflection

- Identify the trial you are currently facing and how it is shaping your faith.

- Confess the temptations that most often target you and the lies beneath them.

- Commit to walking in accountability rather than isolation.

- Prepare by setting spiritual guardrails for the next season of testing.

Prayer

Father, thank You for being near in every trial and faithful in every temptation. Strengthen me when I feel weak and give me wisdom when I am unsure. Teach me to cling to Your promises and reject the enemy's lies. Let every test deepen my faith and let every temptation drive me closer to Christ. In Jesus' name, Amen.

Anchored Together

"Iron sharpens iron, and one man sharpens another." – Proverbs 27:17

You were never meant to walk alone. From the very beginning, God declared,

"IT IS NOT GOOD THAT THE MAN SHOULD BE ALONE"
GENESIS 2:18

. While this verse speaks to the creation of Eve and the covenant of marriage, the principle reaches further, it touches the very fabric of biblical manhood. Isolation is dangerous. The road is too hard, the calling too heavy, and the stakes too high to attempt it solo. God designed men for brotherhood, for shared burdens, sharpened edges, and lifted hands.

The storyline of Scripture confirms this repeatedly. Moses could not hold the staff alone; Aaron and Hur stood beside him and lifted his weary arms. David found courage and loyalty in Jonathan, a brother who strengthened him in God. And Jesus Himself modeled community, surrounding Himself with twelve disciples and sending them out two by two. If the Son of God refused to walk His mission in isolation, how much more do frail and fallen men like us need godly companions?

Why Brotherhood Matters

Gods word paints a vivid picture:

"Two are better than one, because they have a good reward for their toil. For if they fall, one will lift up his fellow."
Ecclesiastes 4:9–10

The value of brotherhood is not just sentimental, it is strategic. Life will bring falls, failures, and fatigue. Brotherhood is God's provision for those moments.

A true brother in Christ provides encouragement when life feels overwhelming. He speaks truth when sin is lurking in the shadows. He offers correction when pride begins to take root. He becomes a source of strength when despair tempts you to give up. In 2024, a Lifeway Research article reported that men who were involved in weekly small groups were more likely to maintain spiritual disciplines and marital health. (Earls, 2024) The difference was not in willpower; it was in community.

Despite the evidence, many men choose isolation. They may not say it outright, but their actions echo the same dangerous lie: "*I've got this.*" Pride tells us we don't need help. Shame convinces us others would reject us if they knew our struggles. Fear whispers that vulnerability is weakness.

But these are lies from the enemy. Peter warns in 1 Peter 5:8, "*Your adversary the devil prowls around like a roaring lion, seeking someone to devour.*" Lions prey on the isolated. The man who walks alone is the man most vulnerable to destruction.

Jesus didn't design His church to be a collection of lone rangers but as a unified body, interconnected, interdependent, and intentional. Real strength is not hiding behind independence but standing with brothers in humble transparency.

Freedom, Not Shame

Accountability is not about shame, it's about freedom. True accountability is voluntary. It means you choose to be known. It is honest, no masks, no pretending. It is biblical, rooted in Scripture, not opinion. And most importantly, it is redemptive, focused on grace, not guilt.

Jesus is not after polished performances. He is after repentant hearts. He longs for honesty, for healing, for men willing to bring the real battles into the light. Authentic accountability doesn't happen in circles where everyone is trying to impress each other, it happens where the gospel is central, and the masks come off.

When a man has the courage to say, *"Here is my sin. Here is my struggle. Here is my brokenness,"* and the brothers around him answer, *"You are still loved. You are not alone. Let's walk this out together,"* that's when freedom begins. That's when chains start to break.

So how do we build this kind of brotherhood? It doesn't happen by accident. It requires intentionality.

First, initiate friendships. Don't wait for others to come to you. Send a text. Invite someone to coffee. Join a Bible study.

> "A MAN WHO HAS FRIENDS MUST HIMSELF BE FRIENDLY."
> *PROVERBS 18:24*

Second, share real struggles. Move past the surface-level talk of weather and sports. Open your heart. Talk about your doubts, your wounds, your temptations

Third, pray together. There is unique power when men pray with and for each other. Scripture reminds us,

> "WHERE TWO OR THREE ARE GATHERED IN MY NAME, THERE AM I
> AMONG THEM."
> *MATTHEW 18:20*

Fourth, serve together. Nothing bonds men like a shared mission. Volunteer. Mentor. Do something for the Kingdom side by side. Brotherhood is strengthened when it moves beyond talk and into action.

Practical accountability needs structure. Here are some questions that foster spiritual honesty:

- Have you been in God's Word consistently this week?
- Have you prayed with and for your wife?
- Have you viewed any pornography or struggled with lust?
- Have you walked in integrity at work and home?
- Have you confessed your sin to God and others?
- Are you harboring any bitterness or unforgiveness?
- Is there anything you're hiding right now?

These are not interrogation tools, they're instruments of transformation. They invite the Spirit to work through honest community.

Biblical Models of Brotherhood

David and Jonathan: Their bond was marked by loyalty, honesty, and covenant love Jonathan risked his life to protect David, even though it meant opposing his own father, King Saul. Their friendship was rooted in a shared faith in God and a commitment to each other's well-being. This kind of loyalty is rare in our individualistic world but desperately needed among men who follow Christ.

Paul and Timothy: Paul served as a spiritual father to Timothy, mentoring and encouraging him in the faith. He entrusted him with leadership, challenged him to be bold, and reminded him of his calling.

This mentorship modeled how older, more seasoned believers are to guide the younger generation in both doctrine and daily life. Paul didn't just teach Timothy how to preach; he showed him how to suffer, persevere, and finish the race well.

Jesus and Peter: Despite Peter's impulsiveness and his denial of Christ, Jesus restored him with grace and a renewed calling. Jesus didn't discard Peter after his failure. Instead, He met him on the shore, fed him, and gave him a mission: *"Feed my sheep."* This moment is a powerful picture of redemptive brotherhood, of picking each other up, speaking truth, and calling one another to deeper purpose after failure.

These relationships were not surface level. They were forged in trials, sustained by truth, and anchored in a shared pursuit of God. In each case, vulnerability, correction, encouragement, and shared mission were present. And they remind us: no man walks faithfully without faithful brothers at his side.

Each of these relationships demonstrates that God uses men to build up other men. Who is your Jonathan? Who are you discipling like Paul? Who are you restoring like Jesus?

When Brotherhood Breaks

Unfortunately, brotherhood is not without risk. Sometimes the deepest wounds come from the very men we trusted. Betrayal, gossip, judgment, abandonment, these can leave lasting scars. But we must not give up on being in community because of broken people. Jesus didn't give up on Peter after he denied Him. Paul didn't stop mentoring because Demas deserted him.

Instead of giving in to the instinct to pull away when hurt or disagreement arises, the call of Christ is higher. We are summoned to forgive freely, to do the hard work of rebuilding broken trust, and to

153

recommit ourselves to the very relationships that shape us. This isn't optional, it's central to the life of Christian brotherhood.

Forgiveness is not weakness; it is obedience. Paul exhorts us,

"BEAR WITH EACH OTHER AND FORGIVE ONE ANOTHER IF ANY OF YOU HAS A GRIEVANCE AGAINST SOMEONE. FORGIVE AS THE LORD FORGAVE YOU."
COLOSSIANS 3:13

Forgiveness is not excusing sin, nor is it forgetting the pain. It is releasing the right to retaliate and entrusting justice to God. In brotherhood, this means we refuse to hold grudges, rehearse offenses, or weaponize past failures. Forgiveness creates the soil where trust can be replanted.

Rebuilding trust is slower and harder, but equally essential. Trust is not restored with words alone; it is proven by consistent, faithful action over time.

"FAITHFUL ARE THE WOUNDS OF A FRIEND."
PROVERBS 27:6

Sometimes rebuilding means having the courage to address what was broken, naming sin honestly, and inviting accountability. Sometimes it means giving the other man space to demonstrate repentance. Either way, rebuilding calls for patience, humility, and a shared commitment to pursue Christ above comfort.

Recommitment is the final piece. Brotherhood is not sustained by feelings but by covenant. Jesus said,

"FOR WHERE TWO OR THREE GATHER IN MY NAME, THERE AM I WITH THEM."
MATTHEW 18:20

That gathering is not always easy. It often requires choosing to stay when it would be simpler to leave. Recommitment means showing up to the table again, praying together again, and linking arms again, even when the scars are still tender. This steadfast presence reflects the God who promises,

When men choose forgiveness, rebuilding, and recommitment, they become living testimonies of the gospel. Every act of reconciliation whispers the greater story, that while we were God's enemies, Christ reconciled us to Himself through the cross. Brotherhood, then, is not about avoiding conflict but about walking through it with grace, truth, and perseverance.

The immeasurable reward of true brotherhood, a deep, supportive, and enduring connection with fellow believers, is unequivocally worth the inherent risk of vulnerability. To truly connect and experience the transformative power of community, one must be willing to open one's heart, share their struggles, and expose their authentic self, even if it means potentially facing pain or rejection.

It is crucial to understand that genuine healing, whether from personal wounds, relational strife, or spiritual struggles, does not happen in isolation. Left alone, pain festers. Isolation magnifies shame, distorts perspective, and often deepens the wound rather than mending it.

On the contrary, healing is a communal process. It blossoms and flourishes within the nurturing environment of a supportive Christian community.

Healing in Community

God never designed us to carry burdens alone. Paul writes,

Healing happens when brothers come alongside us, not to fix us, but to walk with us, to uphold us in prayer, to offer wise counsel, to remind us of truth when lies feel loudest. Their presence becomes a tangible expression of Christ's own love.

The church, as the body of Christ, is meant to be this very sanctuary of healing and restoration. James exhorts believers,

"THEREFORE, CONFESS YOUR SINS TO ONE ANOTHER AND PRAY FOR ONE ANOTHER, THAT YOU MAY BE HEALED"

JAMES 5:16.

Notice the link. Confession leads to prayer, and prayer opens the way to healing. This does not happen in isolation. It happens in the shared life of God's people.

When brothers choose to create safe spaces marked by honesty and grace, wounds begin to close. When a man is listened to without judgment, prayed for with faith, and encouraged with truth, he begins to realize he is not defined by his failures but by Christ's victory. Healing in community doesn't erase scars, it redeems them, transforming them into testimonies of God's faithfulness.

Brotherhood on Mission

In an age marked by disconnection, addiction, and moral confusion, Christian brotherhood is a countercultural revolution. It is a declaration that we will not walk alone.

In 2023, a men's group in Detroit began organizing prayer walks through some of the most violent neighborhoods in the city. Over time, crime dropped, local young men began joining them, and spiritual revival began to spark. The world noticed, not just the boldness, but the brotherhood.

This movement wasn't started by celebrity pastors or mega-church campaigns. It began with ordinary men, teachers, janitors, mechanics, and ex-cons, who were tired of watching their streets crumble under the pressure of hopelessness.

They met weekly, not in polished conference rooms, but in broken-down community centers and cold church basements. They read Scripture, confessed sin, prayed with intensity, and then went out to their streets with oil-stained hands and heaven-stirred hearts.

They didn't just walk for show. They stopped at doorsteps to pray for families. They carried groceries for widows. They shared meals with addicts and offered jobs to young men who had never had one. They weren't trying to go viral; they were trying to go deep.

The change didn't happen overnight, but it happened. Local law enforcement began asking questions. Mothers who had lost sons to violence showed up at prayer meetings. Some drug dealers left the game entirely and joined the movement.

The world is desperate for a vision of manhood that includes brotherhood. Our society glorifies independence and self-made success, but God glorifies unity, humility, and mutual dependence. Real men lock shields. They fight for each other. They lift each other up. They walk together.

If you've been trying to walk this path alone, it's time to stop. You were not made for isolation. You were made for covenant community. The Christian life is not a solo hike; it's a march of brothers under the banner of Christ. Lone wolves become easy prey. But a pack of godly men walking in step with the Spirit, that's an unstoppable force.

Think about Jesus. Even the Son of God surrounded Himself with a band of brothers. Were they flawed? Absolutely. But He invested in them, walked with them, and taught them that mission is always multiplied in fellowship.

The early church was built on brotherhood. Acts 2:42–47 paints a picture of radical community: breaking bread together, praying together, sacrificing for one another. That's the blueprint, the fuel of revival.

The Call to Vulnerability and Strength

To truly thrive as godly men, husbands, and fathers, we must recognize the profound necessity of genuine, Christ-centered brotherhood. This isn't merely about casual camaraderie, but a deep, intentional commitment to one another that fosters spiritual growth and resilience.

It begins with vulnerability. From a young age, most men are conditioned to project strength, to be self-sufficient, to bury their struggles under a stoic exterior.

True strength begins where pride ends. Vulnerability is not weakness; it is the doorway to God's transforming grace.

Take the first step: reach out to a trusted brother in Christ. Share the battles you've been fighting in secret, the temptations that keep circling back, the sin that has weighed heavily on your soul. This kind of transparency requires courage, the kind that trusts God more than appearances, that values holiness more than reputation.

But vulnerability cannot stand alone. It must be joined with accountability. Find a brother who will commit to walk closely with you, to meet weekly, and to share not only burdens but disciplines. Create a rhythm of confession and encouragement.

Be the first to say the words, "*I need help*." This simple act of honesty shatters the chains of secrecy and opens the door for God's Spirit to do what your willpower never could.

Brotherhood that Changes the World

When men humble themselves before God and each other, something powerful happens they move from isolation to intercession, from shame to freedom, from mere survival to spiritual victory. United in Christ, their posture changes.

They don't just endure the battles of life, they overcome them. Their strength is no longer drawn from self, but from the unchanging Word of God and the steadfast encouragement of brothers who refuse to let them fall.

This is biblical manhood: not standing alone, but standing shoulder to shoulder, forged in brotherhood, anchored in Christ.

This interwoven connection creates a brotherhood that is nothing short of transformative. It doesn't stop with the men in the room, it ripples outward. It reshapes families. It breathes new life into weary churches. It can even alter the spiritual landscape of entire cities. History bears witness to this: in places like Detroit, men who chose Christ-centered unity became catalysts for renewal that impacted neighborhoods, workplaces, and communities at large.

Stand Shoulder to Shoulder

You were never meant to walk alone. Jesus Himself modeled life in community. The early church multiplied through it. And today, the call is the same:

- **Embrace vulnerability.**
- **Pursue accountability.**

- **Lock arms in Christ.**

For when men stand together, they become an unstoppable force of grace, brothers forged in the fire, anchored in Christ, and sent as witnesses to the world.

Reflection

- Identify where you are walking alone instead of with godly brothers.

- Confess the areas of struggle or temptation you've been hiding.

- Commit to building deeper relationships of accountability and encouragement this week.

- Decide who you will encourage, challenge, or mentor in their walk with Christ.

Prayer

Father, thank You that I am not called to walk alone. Forgive me for prideful isolation and for hiding in shame. Surround me with brothers who sharpen and strengthen me. Teach me to abide in humility, vulnerability, and truth. Use my life to encourage others and glorify You. In Jesus' name, Amen.

A Call to Action

"Therefore, my beloved brothers, be steadfast, immovable, always abounding in the work of the Lord, knowing that in the Lord your labor is not in vain." 1 Corinthians 15:58

You were not made to drift.

The world's definitions of manhood keep shifting. Society applauds confusion, redefines weakness as strength, and bends its standards with every passing decade. But God's call has never changed.

Biblical manhood is not a trend to try on. It is a divine mandate, bestowed by God, not our broken world. From Adam's first breath in Genesis to the redeemed standing before Christ's throne in Revelation, the call has remained: reflect God's glory.

This is no small calling. It demands everything:

- To reflect His image in character and conduct.

- To guide others with conviction, even when it costs.

- To fight for righteousness against sin and compromise.

- To walk with steadfast faith in trial and temptation.

The mantle of manhood is forged in the fire of obedience, tested in the trenches of daily faithfulness, and proven in unseen places where heaven is watching.

This is the hour to stand. Not tomorrow. Not when life feels easier. Now. This is not optional. This is biblical manhood. This is your call.

Paul's exhortation captures the essence of this . If you have reached this point, it's not by accident. It is a response to a deeper call, a holy invitation to become anchored in Christ.

Anchored in Christ Alone

Storms are inevitable. The question is not if they will come, but whether you will be prepared when they do. Will you be anchored, or will you drift?

When your marriage is strained by seasons of stress or silence, when your children push boundaries or break your heart, when temptation seems relentless and your strength feels spent, when society ridicules your convictions and labels biblical faith as outdated, will you stand?

Hebrews offers this assurance:

"WE HAVE THIS AS A SURE AND STEADFAST ANCHOR OF THE SOUL, A HOPE THAT ENTERS INTO THE INNER PLACE BEHIND THE CURTAIN."
HEBREWS 6:19

That anchor is Christ. He holds when everything else gives way.

Jesus says,

"EVERYONE WHO HEARS THESE WORDS OF MINE AND DOES THEM WILL BE LIKE A WISE MAN WHO BUILT HIS HOUSE ON THE ROCK."
MATTHEW 7:24

The storms beat on both the wise and the foolish. But the difference is the foundation. The foolish man builds on sand, changing opinions, fleeting pleasures, cultural acceptance. The wise man builds on Christ, His Word, His cross, His Spirit.

Anchored men do not merely believe; they obey. They do not merely attend church; they pursue Christ. They are not tossed by every wave of emotion, trend, or hardship. Their roots go deep, their foundation is solid, and their house stands firm.

Throughout this book, we've walked through the many dimensions of biblical manhood:

Identity, you are not a mistake. You were created in God's image, marred by sin, but redeemed by grace.

Leadership is not about power. It is about service. It is about loving your wife with tenderness. It is about guiding your children in truth. It is about leading with courage and compassion.

Purpose, Your life matters. Your work matters. Your worship matters. Every act of obedience is part of a larger Kingdom story.

Perseverance, you will face resistance. But you are not alone. Trials do not destroy anchored men, they refine them.

Legacy, you are shaping generations. Your choices today will echo long after you are gone.

These truths are not abstract theology; they are the blueprints for transformation. Truth without application is wasted. But truth embraced becomes power.

Broken Men, Redeemed for Mission

One of the enemy's most successful lies is this: *"You're not ready."* He whispers that your past disqualifies you, that your weaknesses discredit you, that you must wait until you have it all together. But that day never comes.

Peter denied Jesus three times. With oaths and curses, he swore he had never even known Him. It was a collapse of loyalty at the darkest hour.

Yet on the other side of the resurrection, Jesus sought Peter out. Not to condemn, but to restore. The same man who cowered in fear became the man who stood with boldness at Pentecost, proclaiming Christ with fire and leading 3,000 souls into salvation in a single day.

That is restoration, God not only forgiving failure, but entrusting fresh assignment.

Moses was no different. Before he was a messenger, he was a murderer. Before he was a leader, he was a fugitive, haunted by failure and hiding in the desert.

When God met him at the burning bush, Moses wasn't campaigning for leadership; he was running from it. He argued with God, stacking up excuses: *"I'm not eloquent." "They won't believe me." "Please, send someone else."*

But God, in holy patience, refused to let Moses write himself out of the story. He gave him Aaron, gave him signs, and gave him a mission. And the same insecure stammerer became the prophet who stood unflinching before Pharaoh, thundering, *"Let my people go."*

The fugitive who once ran from Egypt became the leader who brought a nation out of it, who stretched out his hand and watched the Red Sea split, who ascended Sinai and received the law of God face to face.

That's the pattern of grace. Failure does not end your story. In God's hands, it shapes your calling. Peter denied, yet he became a rock in the early church. Moses hid, yet he became a deliverer for God's people. Their weakness turned into the stage for His strength.

And then there's Paul. When we first meet him in Acts 7, he's not preaching the gospel, he's watching Stephen get stoned, guarding the coats of the executioners. By the next chapter, he's breathing threats, hunting Christians, and dragging them to prison. Paul wasn't just misguided; he was a violent enemy of the Church.

But then Jesus showed up. A blinding light. An audible voice. A confrontation that stopped him in his tracks and flipped his world upside down. Saul became Paul. The persecutor became the preacher. The destroyer of the Church became its greatest defender.

From that moment on, Paul lived as a testimony to grace. He wrote letters that now guide the church. He planted new communities of faith. He trained young leaders such as Timothy and Titus.

His record was stained with blood, yet his legacy was filled with the Spirit. That is the gospel. No past is too broken. No sin is too great. No failure is beyond the redeeming power of Christ.

Your failure doesn't disqualify you from God's mission, it positions you for His grace. If Jesus could entrust Peter with His sheep, if God could send Moses back to Egypt, if Christ could turn Saul the persecutor into Paul the preacher, then He can restore you, too.

No past is too broken, no shame too heavy, no sin too great. The same God who rewrote their stories is ready to rewrite yours.

Faithfulness in the Small Things

Truth without obedience is wasted. But consistent obedience builds a godly life.

Practical steps:

- Pray daily, even briefly.
- Read Scripture regularly.
- Lead your home in devotion and blessing.
- Join a brotherhood. Don't walk alone.
- Repent quickly. Stay clean before God.

- Stay consistent. Keep showing up.

Legacy is built daily, not in a day.

Ordinary Faithfulness, Eternal Impact

Consider the story of Edward Kimball, a seemingly ordinary Sunday school teacher in the 1850s. Few today recognize his name, yet his quiet faithfulness changed history. One afternoon, Kimball felt prompted to visit a young shoe salesman named Dwight L. Moody. With trembling hands and a nervous spirit, he shared the gospel with him. That day, Moody surrendered his life to Christ.

Moody went on to become one of the most influential evangelists of the 19th century, reaching millions with the gospel. Through Moody's ministry, others were converted, men like Wilbur Chapman and Billy Sunday, who in turn influenced Mordecai Ham, the preacher who led a young man named Billy Graham to Christ. And Graham, of course, went on to share the gospel with more people than any man in history.

Trace it back, and it all began with one man who chose to be faithful in the small assignment God had given him. Edward Kimball never filled stadiums. He never became a household name. But his legacy still echoes through eternity because he was faithful to share Jesus with one soul.

Fast forward to 2021. A high school janitor in Ohio began quietly praying for students each morning before classes began. He walked the halls, laying hands on lockers, asking God to reveal Himself to a generation overwhelmed by depression, anxiety, and confusion. At first, no one noticed.

But months later, a spontaneous student-led Bible study emerged in the cafeteria. What started with five students grew to over seventy meeting weekly for prayer and Scripture. No spotlight. No microphone. Just faithfulness, and from that faithfulness, revival began to take root.

The Legacy of Faithfulness

You may not be famous. Your name may never trend or be inscribed on a plaque. But heaven notices faithfulness. God sees the dad who comes home from work and leads bedtime prayers. He sees the single man who lives with integrity while waiting on God's timing. He sees the grandfather who writes his testimony for his grandchildren. These are not small things. They are eternal seeds.

Write a note to your child before a big test. Show up to your wife's doctor's appointment even when work is chaotic. Serve in your local church without recognition. Forgive again. Pray again. Hope again. These acts may feel small, but they declare your allegiance to a Kingdom that will never fade.

Don't despise small beginnings. Celebrate every step forward, no matter how small. Progress, not perfection, is the aim. And your faithfulness, compounded over time, will yield a legacy more lasting than applause. Men who are faithful in obscurity become giants in eternity.

The Final Word

Faithfulness is the quiet strength of biblical manhood. It will not trend online. But it will be remembered in heaven.

So stand firm.

Be watchful.

Be strong.

Do all things in love.

That's a legacy that lasts. It's man your family needs, the man God delights to strengthen.

Reflection

- Identify the area of your life that needs to be re-anchored in Christ.

- Confess the lies or distractions that have pulled your heart away from Him.

- Commit to one specific step of obedience you will take this week.

- Decide who you will walk alongside, encouraging them to become anchored as well.

Prayer

Jesus, you are my anchor. When storms rage, when fear rises, when the ground shakes, hold me fast. I surrender all: my past, my plans, my family, my failures. Teach me to abide in steady obedience, to lead with sacrificial love, and to live for Your glory. Make me a man anchored in You, for the sake of my wife, my children, my brothers, and the world around me. Let it all point to You. In Your strong name I pray, Amen

DAILY
DEVOTIONS

Devotions Week 1:

Identity

Before a man can lead his family, love his wife, or disciple his children, he must know who he is. Identity is the foundation for everything. If your identity is insecure, borrowed from the world, or built on performance, every other area of life will suffer. But if your identity is rooted in Christ, you will stand firm, even when storms come.

This week, you'll walk through seven powerful truths:

You are a new creation.

Your past no longer defines you.

You are adopted.

You are a son, not a stranger.

You are crucified with Christ.

Your old life is gone.

You are God's workmanship, made with purpose.

God delights in you; He doesn't just tolerate you.

You are rooted in grace.

You don't earn God's favor.

These truths aren't self-help affirmations, they're gospel realities. This week will renew your mind, soften your heart, and re-center your life on the grace of God.

Day 1: A New Creation

"Therefore, if anyone is in Christ, he is a new creation. The old has passed away; behold, the new has come." – 2 Corinthians 5:17

In Christ, your past no longer has the power to define you or your marriage. The moment you trusted in Jesus, your old self was crucified with Him, and a new creation was born. That truth is not only for your personal salvation but also for every part of your life. It shapes how you love your wife, how you lead your home, and how you carry yourself as a man of God.

Failures, regrets, and wounds may still whisper to you, but they do not get the final word. The blood of Christ has spoken a greater word: forgiven, free, redeemed, and restored. God does not label you by your worst mistakes or past sins. He calls you by your name.

You are not chained to repeat the cycles of brokenness that came before you. By God's grace, you can walk in humility, forgive without holding back, serve with a willing heart, and love with a depth that reflects Christ Himself.

Your marriage is not sustained by your perfection. It is sustained by Christ's redeeming power at work in you. When you stumble, His grace restores. When your love feels insufficient, His love overflows through you.

So, live today as the man you truly are in Christ, a new creation. Step forward with confidence, not in yourself but in the One who makes all things new. Let your marriage be a living testimony of God's transforming grace, a reflection of freedom, hope, and redemption.

Prayer

Father, thank You that through Jesus Christ I am made completely new. My past mistakes, failures, and shortcomings no longer define me. Help me to live daily in the reality of this new identity You have given me, not based on my past, my performance, or the opinions of others, but firmly anchored in Your love and grace. Teach me to see myself through Your eyes, as forgiven, redeemed, and empowered to walk in freedom. Amen.

Action Step

Take a quiet moment before the Lord and write down a past sin, regret, or false label that has weighed on your heart. It could be a word like "unworthy," "failure," or "not enough." Or is it a memory of choices you wish you could undo? Look at what you've written, acknowledge its weight, and then remember God's promise:

"IF WE CONFESS OUR SINS, HE IS FAITHFUL AND JUST TO FORGIVE US OUR SINS AND TO CLEANSE US FROM ALL UNRIGHTEOUSNESS"
1 JOHN 1:9

Now cross it out boldly and write over it: **"NEW CREATION."** This is not wishful thinking but the truth of Scripture:

"IF ANYONE IS IN CHRIST, HE IS A NEW CREATION. THE OLD HAS PASSED AWAY; BEHOLD, THE NEW HAS COME"
2 CORINTHIANS 5:17

Place that reminder where you will see it often. Each time you read it, remember your past does not define you. In Christ, you are forgiven, restored, and free to live in His grace.

Day 2: Adopted as Sons

---

*"For you did not receive the spirit of slavery to fall back into fear,
but you have received the Spirit of adoption as sons, by whom we cry,
'Abba! Father!'– Romans 8:15*

You are not a slave to fear. You are not chained to failure. You are not defined by performance. You are a beloved son of the living God. This is the truth that sets you free from the lies that once held you captive.

Through Christ, you have been rescued not only from sin but also from separation and shame. You are no longer on the outside looking in. You have been welcomed fully into God's family, embraced by His open arms and secured by His unshakable love.

As His child, you have been given intimate access to the Father's heart. You are not kept at a distance. You can draw near in prayer, worship, and trust. Along with that access comes a rich inheritance that cannot be lost or stolen. This is your identity now. It's not earned by effort but bestowed by grace. It isn't fragile but forever secure in Christ.

As His son, you walk with a new name and a new nature, marked by love, acceptance, and strength. Let this truth be the bedrock of your leadership as a man. Let it guide your words when you speak to your wife and children. Let it shape your decisions when pressures mount. Let it steady your heart as you shepherd those entrusted to your care.

You belong to Him, and in that belonging you find the freedom, identity, and strength you need for the road ahead.

Prayer

Father, thank You for adopting me into Your family and calling me Your child. Help me to live each day in the boldness and security that come from knowing I am completely loved and accepted by You. Teach me to lead my family with confidence, humility, and grace, reflecting the honor and responsibility of being Your son. Let Your love be my foundation and strength in every challenge and decision. May my life bring glory to Your name as I walk faithfully in the identity You have given me. Amen.

Action Step

Take a moment to stand before a mirror and speak truth over yourself. Look into your own eyes and declare with confidence: *"I am a child of God. I am His son. I am fully loved."* Do not rush these words. Say them slowly, letting them move from your lips into your heart. These are not empty affirmations but eternal realities purchased by the blood of Christ.

As you speak them, allow the Spirit to remind you that your worth does not come from performance, success, or the opinions of others. It comes from your Father who has called you His own. Let this identity anchor you as you step into the day. Show up as a man who knows he is chosen, forgiven, and loved beyond measure.

Day 3: Crucified with Christ

"I have been crucified with Christ. It is no longer I who live, but Christ who lives in me. And the life I now live in the flesh I live by faith in the Son of God, who loved me and gave himself for me." – *Galatians 2:20*

Your old self, the one bound by sin, fear, and self-will, was crucified with Jesus on the cross. That way of living, driven by pride, control, and the endless pursuit of approval, no longer has power over you. The man you once were has been put to death, and in his place, Christ has made you new.

Now Christ lives in you through His Spirit. He is not distant. He is present and active. He guides your thoughts. He shapes your choices. He aligns your goals with His eternal purpose. To surrender to Him is not bondage. It is the only road to true freedom. The cycle of striving, performing, and trying to earn what only God can give is broken.

This is freedom with purpose. It rests on God's grace and draws on His power. It is freedom to love your wife without fear. It is freedom to lead your family with humility. It is freedom to walk each day with confidence, knowing you are never alone. Each step is fueled by His love, His strength, and His wisdom.

Today, embrace that freedom. Do not return to old chains. Let the Spirit of Christ lead your heart and guide your actions. Walk boldly in the calling He has given you. Live as a man crucified with Christ, yet more alive than ever because His Spirit works within you.

Prayer

Jesus, I surrender my own plans and agendas to You. Help me to live each day in a way that reflects Your heart and Your purposes. Lead me with Your wisdom, guide me by Your Spirit, and let Your life flow through mine. Teach me to relinquish control and trust fully in Your perfect plan. May my thoughts, words, and actions be shaped by Your love and grace today. Use me as an instrument of Your peace and obedience. Amen.

Action Step

Take a quiet moment to reflect on your life and identify one area where you are still clinging to control. It might be a relationship, a decision about work, a financial burden, or a hidden fear about the future. Write it down honestly before God, naming it for what it is. Then pray, inviting Jesus to take full leadership in that place.

After you pray, choose one small and specific step to act on today as an expression of surrender. It could mean releasing worry in prayer instead of replaying it in your mind, calling a trusted brother for counsel, or refusing to rush ahead of God's timing. Whatever it looks like, take that step with faith, believing that His strength is made perfect in your weakness.

Day 4: God's Workmanship

"For we are his workmanship, created in Christ Jesus for good works, which God prepared beforehand, that we should walk in them." – Ephesians 2:10

You are not an accident or an afterthought. You are God's masterpiece, created with care and intention, wonderfully crafted with unique gifts, passions, and a specific calling. The God who formed the stars also formed you with a purpose that fits perfectly within His eternal plan.

Your life is not a collection of random events. Every step you take, every responsibility you carry, and every role you fulfill is part of God's design. As a husband, a father, and a servant, you hold assignments entrusted to you by God Himself. These are not small or secondary roles, but sacred opportunities to reflect His image and advance His kingdom.

This truth transforms ordinary, everyday tasks into acts of worship. When you lead your family in prayer, when you love your wife with patience, when you work diligently at your job, or when you serve faithfully in your church, you are living out your calling. What may seem routine or unnoticed in the moment carries eternal weight in the eyes of God.

When you embrace this identity, everything changes. Your perspective shifts from duty to destiny. Each moment becomes infused with meaning, not because of your strength, but because of the God who designed it all. Today, choose to abide in that truth. See yourself as God's masterpiece, called for such a time as this, and live with confidence that your life reflects His glory.

Prayer

Lord, thank You for creating me with intention and purpose. Help me to recognize and embrace these blessings each day. Guide me as I seek to walk faithfully in the good works You have prepared for me. Use my life to impact my family, my community, and Your kingdom. Empower me to serve with joy, humility, and diligence, trusting that You will multiply even the smallest efforts. Amen.

Action Step

Take a few minutes to write down three specific gifts, talents, or passions that God has placed in your life. They may be skills like teaching, organizing, or encouraging, or simple passions such as cooking, fixing things, or listening well. Remember that every gift, big or small, has been entrusted to you by your Creator for His glory and the good of others.

Next to each gift, write one practical way you can use it this week to serve. It could be encouraging a family member with a kind word, helping a neighbor with a task, mentoring someone at church, or simply setting an example of integrity at work. Commit to putting these into action and trust that God will multiply your faithfulness. As you pour out what He has given you, you will see His grace flow through you to bless others.

Day 5: He Delights in You

"The Lord your God is in your midst, a mighty one who will save;
He will rejoice over you with gladness; He will quiet you by His love;
He will exult over you with loud singing." – Zephaniah 3:17

You are not merely accepted; you are celebrated by God. He does not tolerate you out of obligation or duty. He delights in you because He loves you sincerely and chooses to. The God of the universe, who spoke creation into being, rejoices over you as His beloved child.

You do not have to earn His approval through performance or hide your weaknesses out of fear of rejection. God's joy over you is abundant and unchanging, and this truth defines your identity far more than your past mistakes or present struggles.

When you embrace this reality, it transforms the way you see yourself. No longer do you live as a man striving for worth, but as one who already has it in Christ. From that place of security, you can give yourself away in love.

Let God's delight in you overflow into your marriage and family. Love your wife with the same joy and acceptance that the Father shows you. Lead your children with patience and encouragement, reflecting His delight in them as well.

As you rest in His joy, you will love more freely, forgive more readily, and lead with a heart anchored in grace and confidence. God's delight is both your foundation and the fuel that empowers you to reflect His character in every area of life.

Prayer

Father, help me to fully receive and embrace Your joy over me. Let the truth of Your delight sink deep into my heart and transform the way I see myself. Teach me to live from this place of acceptance, not striving, so that Your love flows freely through me. May Your joy overflow in my relationships, especially in how I love my family and lead with grace and patience. Thank You for choosing me and celebrating me just as I am. Amen.

Action Step

Set aside five quiet minutes today with no phone, no noise, and no distractions. Sit in a comfortable place, close your eyes, and slowly repeat this truth to yourself: *"God delights in me."* Let the words sink deep into your heart. This is not based on your performance, but on His unchanging love. Remember Zephaniah 3:17: *"He will take great delight in you; in his love he will no longer rebuke you, but will rejoice over you with singing."*

As you breathe deeply and rest in this truth, carry it into your day. Notice how it shapes your mindset, your patience, and the way you speak to those closest to you. When stress rises or frustration surfaces, return to this anchor: *"God delights in me."* From that place of secure love, you are freed to delight in others, especially your family.

Day 6: Rooted in Grace

"He saved us, not because of works done by us in righteousness, but according to his own mercy, by the washing of regeneration and renewal of the Holy Spirit, whom he poured out on us richly through Jesus Christ our Savior" – *Titus 3:5-6*

Your relationship with God is not founded on your performance or ability to meet standards. It begins and continues because of His abundant mercy and grace. God saved you not because you earned it, but because His heart overflows with compassion.

When you stumble, fail, or fall short in your roles as a husband or father, His grace is there to lift you up, restore you, and empower you to keep going. You do not need to hide in shame or pretend to be perfect. You can stand secure in the knowledge that God's love does not waver with your performance.

Leading a family is challenging, and it is easy to grow weary or impatient. Grace provides the patience, love, and strength you need to persevere. It equips you to love sacrificially, to forgive quickly, and to lead faithfully.

Each day is a new opportunity to walk in that grace. As receive God's mercy, let it overflow into your marriage, your parenting, and your daily interactions. Extend to others the same grace that has been given to you, and you will find yourself strengthened by His Spirit in every area of life.

Prayer

Lord, thank You for saving me by Your amazing grace. I recognize that I could never earn Your love or forgiveness, and I don't deserve it. Yet, you chose to rescue me anyway. Help me to remember that Your grace is sufficient for every weakness. Teach me to extend that same grace to my family, to be patient, forgiving, and loving, even when it's difficult. Let Your mercy shape my heart and guide my actions so that I reflect Your kindness and compassion in all my relationships. Amen.

Action Step

Take time to reflect on something you have struggled to forgive yourself for, whether a mistake, a failure, or a regret that still weighs heavy. Write it down honestly, bringing it into the light of God's presence.

Remind yourself that the cross covers even this, and God's grace is greater than your deepest wound.

Next, turn outward. Think of someone in your life who may be carrying a similar weight of shame, regret, or hurt. Ask God to give you the courage to reach out with kindness, encouragement, or a listening ear. Extend the same grace that you have received, remembering Jesus' words:

"FREELY YOU HAVE RECEIVED; FREELY GIVE"
MATTHEW 10:8

In doing so, you not only walk in forgiveness yourself but also become a vessel of God's healing in the life of another.

Day 7: Identity vs Performance

"Nevertheless, do not rejoice in this, that the spirits are subject to you, but rejoice that your names are written in heaven." Luke 10:20

We often believe that our value is tied to what we do for God, how well we perform, or the impact we make. It is tempting to measure ourselves by our work, our accomplishments, or the opinions of others. Yet the truth is far deeper and more freeing. Your worth is not based on your achievements or failures, your career success, or even the extent of your service.

Your identity is anchored in the unchanging reality that you are fully known, deeply loved, and completely accepted by God. This identity does not shift with circumstances, and it cannot be taken away by mistakes, struggles, or setbacks. It is a secure foundation that rests entirely on His grace.

When you rest in this truth, you can live with freedom and confidence. You no longer need to strive endlessly to prove yourself or fear that you will fall short. Instead, you are free to respond to God's love with gratitude, humility, and faithful obedience.

This perspective changes everything. Your work becomes service, not striving. Your relationships become opportunities to reflect God's love, not arenas for proving your worth. And your life as a whole becomes a testimony of the grace that secures your identity in Him.

Prayer

Jesus, thank You that my identity is secure and unshakable in You. Help me to rest fully in Your perfect love and acceptance, rather than in my achievements or the approval of others. Guard my heart against the temptation to seek my worth in performance, success, or what I do. Remind me daily that I am deeply known and beloved by You, just as I am. Teach me to live from this place of freedom and grace, so that my life reflects Your peace and joy. Amen.

Action Step

Choose one hour today to step away from your phone, computer, and every digital distraction. Release the urge to check notifications, answer messages, or fill the silence with noise. In this space, lay down the pressure to produce, perform, or prove yourself. Instead, rest in the truth that your identity is secure in Christ. Remember His promise:

"BE STILL, AND KNOW THAT I AM GOD"
PSALM 46:10

As you sit in that stillness, breathe deeply and let God's Word remind you that you are fully accepted and loved apart from your work or accomplishments. Meditate on His promises, perhaps repeating quietly, *"The Lord is my shepherd; I shall not want"* (Psalm 23:1). Allow His love to refresh your heart, renew your mind, and restore your strength for the day ahead.

Devotions Week 2:

Anchored in Marriage

Marriage is not merely a human contract; it is a sacred covenant designed and instituted by God. From the beginning. When a man and woman are joined in marriage, it is more than a legal agreement, it is a covenant before God. At the very heart of this covenant is the call for husbands to love, lead, and serve their wives in a way that reflects Jesus Christ's own relationship with the Church.

In a world that often views marriage as temporary and self-centered, God's Word offers a countercultural vision. True love is not based on convenience or fleeting emotion; it is covenantal, steadfast, and sacrificial. The love between husband and wife is meant to be a living testimony of Christ's unwavering love for His bride. When husbands embrace this calling, marriage becomes more than companionship—it becomes a picture of the gospel itself.

This week's devotions will guide you to anchor your marriage in Christ and to live out your covenant with renewed faithfulness. You will be challenged and encouraged to:

Reflect Christ's sacrificial love in your daily choices.

Strengthen intimacy—emotional, spiritual, and physical.

Cultivate habits of communication, forgiveness, and joy.

Reclaim the beauty of serving and honoring your wife.

As you walk through these truths, remember that strong marriages are not built in moments of ease but in the daily faithfulness of ordinary days. Every choice to love, to serve, and to forgive becomes a brick in the foundation of a lasting covenant. Anchored in Christ, your marriage can withstand storms, flourish in joy, and shine as a witness of God's unbreakable love.

Day 8: Loving as Christ

"Husbands, love your wives, as Christ loved the church and gave himself up for her." – Ephesians 5:25

Jesus set the standard for love. It was not a sentimental or shallow affection but a sacrificial and servant-hearted devotion. To love as Christ means putting your spouse's needs before your own, leading by serving, forgiving quickly, and choosing tenderness even when you are tired, frustrated, or misunderstood.

This kind of love calls you to lay down pride, selfishness, and the desire to be right. It is a commitment to pursue your spouse's good above your own comfort, echoing the example of Jesus, who humbled Himself and gave everything for His bride.

True love is lived out in the everyday moments. It looks like listening before speaking, offering grace after mistakes, and showing affection when it is least deserved. These small but intentional choices reveal a heart that is surrendered to Christ and willing to love as He loves.

When you love in this way, you invite Christ's presence and healing into your marriage. Even ordinary days and difficult seasons become opportunities to reflect His transforming love, drawing you and your spouse closer to one another and to Him.

Prayer

Lord, teach me to love my wife as You loved the Church, with deep sacrifice, unwavering patience, and abundant grace. Fill my heart with Your compassion so that I may reflect Your love in every word, action, and decision at home. Remind me that true love means laying down my pride, serving with joy, and forgiving quickly, even when it is hard. Help me put her needs before my own, seeking her good and her growth above my comfort. Mold me into a husband whose actions speak louder than words, whose life points her to You, and whose love creates a safe and nurturing home. Let every moment be an opportunity to honor You through how I love her. Amen.

Action Step

Take a moment this week to look your wife in the eye and ask with genuine humility, *"How can I love you better this week?"* Do not ask casually or out of habit, but with a heart ready to listen. When she answers, give her your full attention without interrupting or defending yourself. Write down what she shares, no matter how small it may seem, and bring it before God in prayer.

Then, make it your mission to act on her words with intentionality. If she longs for more quality time, clear space in your schedule. If she needs help carrying a burden, step in willingly. If she desires encouragement, speak life over her daily. In doing these things, you mirror Christ's love for the church, a love that listens, serves, and sacrifices. Your wife will not just hear your love; she will see it lived out in tangible ways.

Day 9: Two Become One

"Therefore, a man shall leave his father and his mother and hold fast to his wife, and they shall become one flesh." – Genesis 2:24

From the very beginning, God's design for marriage was unity. It was never intended to be mere cohabitation or the sharing of responsibilities. Marriage is a covenant of deep spiritual, emotional, and physical oneness that reflects God's own character and love. In Genesis 2:24 we read, *"Therefore a man shall leave his father and his mother and hold fast to his wife, and they shall become one flesh."* This oneness is a sacred bond, mirroring the unity within the Trinity, and it points the world to the faithfulness and love of God.

Yet unity in marriage is not automatic. It must be pursued, nurtured, and guarded with intention. The enemy seeks to divide what God has joined together, and distractions of life can slowly erode intimacy. Guard your marriage not only from obvious threats such as temptation, unresolved conflict, or busyness, but also from subtle dangers like complacency, unspoken resentments, or neglecting emotional connection. Unity is lost more often through slow drift than sudden collapse.

True oneness is built daily. It grows through intentional love, patient listening, open communication, and the shared rhythm of prayer. It deepens when you choose forgiveness over bitterness, when you make time to delight in one another, and when you walk together in obedience to Christ. Ecclesiastes 4:12 reminds us, *"A cord of three strands is not quickly broken."* With Christ at the center, your unity is strengthened and sustained.

Prayer

Father, thank You for the precious gift of my wife and the sacred covenant of marriage. Help us to walk together in unity, pursuing deeper spiritual, emotional, and physical oneness. Let nothing and no one divide what You have joined together. Strengthen our bond daily through the power of Your Spirit and teach us to forgive, serve, and cherish one another as Christ loves the Church. Guard our hearts from complacency and distractions and fill our home with Your peace and joy. May our marriage be a testimony of Your love to the world. Amen.

Action Step

Make it a priority this week to set aside intentional, uninterrupted time with your wife. Whether it is a date night, a walk around the neighborhood, or a quiet dinner at home, choose a setting where you can truly reconnect. Put away distractions, silence your phone, and give her your full attention. This is not just about spending time together but about showing her that she is worth your focus and presence.

Use this time to laugh freely, to listen deeply, and to share your hearts without rush. Let your words build her up and let your presence remind her that she is cherished. Guard these moments as a sacred investment in your marriage. As Scripture says,

"What therefore God has joined together, let not man separate"
Mark 10:9

When you honor your wife with intentional time, you strengthen the bond of oneness God designed for your marriage.

Day 10: Honoring Your Wife

"Likewise, husbands, live with your wives in an understanding way, showing honor to the woman as the weaker vessel, since they are heirs with you of the grace of life, so that your prayers may not be hindered." — 1 Peter 3:7

Biblical honor is not merely about politeness or occasional romantic gestures. It is about recognizing the God-given dignity, value, and worth of your wife every day. Honor is not seasonal or occasional, but a posture of the heart that shapes how you see and treat her in every circumstance.

To honor your wife means listening with genuine empathy, seeking to understand her heart, and making her feel truly heard and valued. It means always speaking of her with respect, whether she is present or not, and refusing to let criticism or disrespect take root in your words.

Honor is lived out in small, consistent acts of kindness and intentionality. It is prioritizing her needs, supporting her dreams, and protecting her reputation. When you honor your wife in this way, you reflect Christ's love for His Church and build a foundation of trust, security, and strength in your marriage.

Prayer

Lord, help me to see my wife as You see her, a treasured daughter and co-heir of Your grace. Forgive me for the times I have failed to honor her in my thoughts, words, or actions. Shape my heart to treat her with the reverence, respect, and care You command. Teach me to be mindful in my interactions, to build her up, and to protect her dignity. Let my love be a daily testimony to Your transforming grace, so that others might see Christ in our marriage. Empower me by Your Spirit to love, cherish, and honor her all the days of my life. Amen.

Action Step

Take intentional time today to write your wife a heartfelt note of appreciation. Do not settle for general words, be specific. Reflect on something she has done recently that you are truly grateful for, whether it was an act of kindness, a sacrifice she made, or the way she cared for your family. Write in a way that lets her know you see her, value her, and honor her deeply from the heart.

Place the note somewhere she will discover it naturally, on her pillow, in her Bible, or beside her morning coffee. As you leave it, pray that God uses your words to bless her spirit and strengthen her heart. A simple note, when written with sincerity, can become a powerful reminder of Christ's love expressed through you, her husband.

Day 11: A Cord of Three

"Though one may be overpowered, two can defend themselves. A cord of three strands is not quickly broken." – Ecclesiastes 4:12

A truly strong marriage is more than just the union of two people. It is a covenant partnership grounded in Christ. Ecclesiastes 4:12 reminds us, *"Though one may be overpowered, two can defend themselves. A cord of three strands is not quickly broken."* When Jesus is the third strand in your marriage, you no longer depend only on your own patience, love, or wisdom. Instead, you draw from His limitless strength, and He binds your lives together with a bond that cannot be broken.

His grace empowers you to forgive when forgiveness feels impossible, to persevere through difficult seasons, and to love beyond your natural limits. Every marriage faces conflict, but Christ offers healing when tension rises. Every marriage walks through moments of confusion, but Christ gives clarity and peace. Every marriage experiences the routines of daily life, and it is Christ who renews purpose in even the simplest tasks.

Marriage is not simply about sharing a home, managing responsibilities, or raising children together. It is about living as one flesh, united in spirit and mission. When you and your wife intentionally draw near to Christ together, your unity is strengthened.

This kind of marriage shines in a watching world. When others see patience, grace, and sacrificial love flowing between you and your wife, they see Christ at work. Your relationship becomes a visible witness to the gospel, showing that God is still in the business of redeeming, restoring, and sustaining love. Keep Jesus at the center, and your marriage will not only endure, it will flourish for His glory.

Prayer

Jesus, be the center and foundation of our marriage. Help us to rely on You more than ourselves in every season, through joys, trials, and ordinary days. Strengthen our bond with Your presence and fill our home with Your peace and wisdom. Teach us to forgive as You forgive, to love as You love, and to persevere with hope, always drawing closer to You and to each other. Let our marriage reflect Your glory and grace so that others may see Your transforming power at work in us. Amen.

Action Step

Establish a simple but consistent weekly prayer time with your wife. Choose a regular moment, perhaps at the start or end of the week, when you can come together before God, even if only for a few minutes. Make it a habit that is easy to keep. Pray aloud, hold hands, and invite the Lord into the center of your marriage.

Use this time to lift up your marriage, your family, and each other's personal needs. Ask Christ to guide your steps, protect your home, and strengthen your love. As you do, you will find your hearts growing closer, not only to one another but to Him. This simple rhythm can become a sacred anchor that steadies your relationship in the unchanging love of God.

Day 12: Forgiveness in Marriage

"Bear with each other and forgive one another if any of you has a grievance against someone. Forgive as the Lord forgave you." – *Colossians 3:13*

Forgiveness is the heartbeat of a healthy marriage. It's not a one-time event but an ongoing lifestyle that sustains and strengthens your relationship. Even small offenses, careless words, or moments of impatience can gradually grow into large walls if left unresolved. Bitterness acts like poison to intimacy, slowly eroding trust and closeness, while forgiveness restores and rebuilds connection.

Humility is essential for this process. Be quick to admit when you are wrong, and just as quick to extend forgiveness when your spouse falls short. A marriage anchored in grace and forgiveness creates an atmosphere where healing and unity can flourish.

When you choose daily forgiveness, you mirror Christ's love. You restore hope, deepen intimacy, and invite God's blessing into your home. This kind of forgiveness is not weakness but strength, and it reflects the heart of the gospel to a watching world.

Prayer

Father, help me to forgive as You have so freely forgiven me. Soften my heart and remove any trace of bitterness, pride, or resentment. Teach me to lead with grace and humility in every moment, especially when I feel wounded or unheard. Fill me with Your Spirit so that my first instinct is to seek reconciliation and extend mercy, just as You do. Make my marriage a place where forgiveness flows easily, bringing healing and renewed intimacy. Let our relationship be a testimony of Your transforming love and grace. Amen.

Action Step

Set aside time today to have an honest and loving conversation with your wife. Choose a moment when you are both free from distractions so you can give one another your full attention. Speak gently and with humility, addressing any unresolved hurt or tension that may have lingered between you. Share your heart with care, not to win an argument, but to seek understanding and healing.

As you talk, listen closely to her words and feelings. Ask for forgiveness where it is needed, and extend forgiveness freely when she seeks it from you. End the conversation with prayer if possible, inviting God to cover your marriage with His grace. By choosing to walk in forgiveness, you open the door to renewed closeness and a deeper unity anchored in Christ.

Day 13: Servant Leadership

"For even the Son of Man came not to be served but to serve, and to give his life as a ransom for many." – Mark 10:45

Biblical leadership is never about dominance, control, or demanding your own way. It is about humble service. Jesus Himself modeled this truth when He said,

"THE SON OF MAN CAME NOT TO BE SERVED BUT TO SERVE, AND TO GIVE HIS LIFE AS A RANSOM FOR MANY"
MARK 10:45

To lead your family well means being the first to sacrifice, the first to listen, and the first to repent. True leadership puts your wife's needs above your comfort and your children's well-being above your personal agenda

This posture communicates security to your wife and stability to your children. It shows them that leadership in God's design is never about power, but about love expressed through service.

This kind of leadership creates an atmosphere of safety, trust, and unity. When you consistently serve, your home becomes a place where your wife feels cherished and your children feel valued. They learn that strength is shown not in control, but in sacrifice. They experience firsthand the love of Christ through your daily choices.

In choosing to lead through service, you embody the heart of Jesus. Your leadership leaves behind a legacy of love that will impact generations. Your children will remember how you served, and they will carry that example into their own marriages and families. This is leadership that lasts, because it is rooted in the eternal love of Christ.

Prayer

Jesus, teach me to lead like You, through service, sacrifice, and humility. Give me a heart that seeks the good of my family above my own desires. Fill my home with Your love, peace, and presence so that my leadership reflects Your heart. Help me to lay down my preferences and comfort, and instead, serve with joy and willingness, even when no one sees. Shape me into a leader who inspires trust, safety, and hope by following Your example. May my actions speak louder than words, and may my life point my family to You every day. Amen.

Action Step

Choose to do something today that requires real sacrifice of time, comfort, or personal preference. It may be taking on an extra chore so your wife can rest, setting aside your own plans so you can be present with your children, or listening attentively when you would rather relax. Find ways to serve your family in ways that truly meet their needs.

Do it quietly, without drawing attention or expecting thanks. Remember the words of Jesus in Mark 10:45: *"For even the Son of Man came not to be served but to serve, and to give his life as a ransom for many."* When you serve in this spirit, your actions reflect the servant-hearted love of Christ and plant seeds of grace that will strengthen your home.

Day 14: Cherish Her Deeply

---

*"Let your fountain be blessed, and rejoice in the wife of your youth,
a lovely deer, a graceful doe. Let her breasts fill you at all times with
delight; be intoxicated always in her love." Proverbs 5:18–19*

To cherish your wife is to actively value, honor, and nurture her heart every day. It is more than occasional romantic gestures or special celebrations. Cherishing is the daily commitment to speak life into her, to encourage her, and to keep the flame of love burning strong no matter how many years you have been married

To cherish her is to remind her often and sincerely that she is seen, treasured, and beautiful. It is loving her not only for what she does but for who she is as a unique, God-crafted woman. Proverbs 31:29 declares, *"Many women have done excellently, but you surpass them all."* Your words and actions should regularly affirm her worth, not as a duty, but as a joyful expression of your love and gratitude.

Cherishing also requires intentional choices. It may be as simple as pausing to listen fully, offering a word of encouragement when she feels weary, or protecting time together in the midst of a busy schedule. It is showing her that she is your priority, second only to God. Small daily acts of care and affirmation build a pattern of love that strengthens your marriage over time.

When you choose to cherish your wife in this way, you create an atmosphere where love can flourish. Your marriage becomes a safe and joyful place, marked by trust, tenderness, and unity. In this, you reflect Christ's deep affection for His Bride, the Church, and you honor God's design for marriage. Cherishing is not a one-time decision but a lifelong calling, one that blesses your wife and glorifies the Lord.

Prayer

Lord, open my eyes to the beauty and blessing of my wife. Help me to see her as You see her, precious, valued, and deeply loved. Teach me to cherish her as You cherish the Church, with joy, sacrifice, and deep affection. Fill my heart with gratitude for who she is, not just for what she does. Give me the wisdom to nurture her spirit and the intentionality to make her feel seen and celebrated every day. May my words and actions continually affirm her worth and bring delight to her heart. Amen.

Action Step

Take time today to tell your wife three specific things you genuinely love and appreciate about her. Think carefully about your words so they go beyond general compliments. Mention qualities you admire, actions she has taken recently, or the ways she blesses your family. Speak with sincerity and affection, looking her in the eye so she knows you truly mean what you say.

As you do, notice the joy that rises in her heart and the way encouragement softens the atmosphere of your home. Words have the power to build up, and when spoken with love, they strengthen the bond of marriage. Let this become a regular practice, a simple rhythm of cherishing your wife, and you will see how consistent encouragement deepens intimacy and trust.

Devotions Week 3:

Intentional Fatherhood

Fatherhood is one of the most sacred callings a man can carry. It's not passive or accidental; it is intentional and deeply spiritual. A father is not simply raising children but shaping future men and women of God. Your influence is not limited to the present moment; it echoes into generations. The words you speak, the choices you make, and the example you set will leave a mark on your children's faith and character long after they are grown.

This week we focus on building a fatherhood that mirrors the heart of God. Discipline must reflect the love of our Heavenly Father, who disciplines those He loves, not to punish but to shape and restore.

Intentional fatherhood goes beyond simply being present in the home. It requires spiritual engagement. It means praying with and for your children, speaking blessing over their lives, and modeling what repentance looks like when you fall short. When your children see humility and forgiveness in you, they learn firsthand the grace of God. When they hear you pray, they learn the importance of walking with Him. When they watch you live with integrity, they see what it means to live as a disciple of Christ.

Fatherhood is a daily calling that requires endurance, love, and faith. The moments may seem ordinary—bedtime prayers, car rides, family meals—but they are the soil where faith takes root. More than lessons taught, faith is caught in the rhythms of life. As you faithfully sow seeds of truth, love, and grace, you prepare your children to grow into men and women who know the love of their Heavenly Father and are equipped to walk in His ways.

Day 15: Train Them in the Way

"Train up a child in the way he should go; even when he is old he will not depart from it." Proverbs 22:6

Parenting is far more than managing behavior. It is about shaping character and cultivating a heart for God. Proverbs 22:6 reminds us, *"Train up a child in the way he should go; even when he is old he will not depart from it."* Training is not a one-time event. It is a lifelong and intentional investment. To train is to guide, instruct, encourage, and model godly living day after day. This calling requires consistency, patience, grace, and a long-term vision for your child's future in Christ.

Children are not just future adults; they are present disciples in training. They need your time, attention, and spiritual leadership. Correction alone will not shape their character. What truly forms their hearts is direction anchored in truth, coupled with the love and example you provide. When discipline is joined with encouragement, when guidance is paired with compassion, children learn that following Christ is not about rules but about relationship.

Your children are watching you more closely than you realize. What they see in you is what they are most likely to reflect. Your faith, integrity, humility, and love leave a mark deeper than your words ever can. Let your life be the lesson. Show them what it looks like to forgive quickly, to serve joyfully, to pray faithfully, and to stand firm in truth.

Parenting is discipleship in its most personal form. Each ordinary moment, mealtime conversations, bedtime prayers, car rides, and even moments of failure, is an opportunity to shape your children's view of God.

Prayer

Father, help me to be a faithful and intentional guide to my children. Give me wisdom to know how to lead them, patience to walk with them through their struggles, and a deep, unwavering love that reflects Your heart. Help me to model a life anchored in Your truth and grace and let my actions and words point them consistently toward You. Shape their hearts and character through my example and empower me to train them up in the way they should go. May our home be a place where faith, kindness, and integrity are lived out every day. Amen.

Action Step

Choose one specific value or biblical truth to focus on with your children this week. It might be honesty, forgiveness, kindness, or prayer. Make it something simple and clear so they can easily understand and remember it. Look for natural moments during the day to point it out, talk about it, and pray together. Let them see how that truth connects to God's Word and to everyday life.

As you model this truth in your own actions and decisions, your children will notice. When you choose forgiveness over anger, kindness over harshness, or prayer over worry, you are planting living seeds of faith in their hearts. Over time, these small, consistent moments shape their understanding of God and guide them in becoming men and women who walk in His ways.

Day 16: Bring Them Up in the Lord

"Fathers, do not provoke your children to anger, but bring them up in the discipline and instruction of the Lord." – Ephesians 6:4

As fathers, we are not called to dominate or dictate. We are called to disciple and nurture our children's hearts. True discipline is not about punishment but about purposeful training, guiding our kids with wisdom and love. Instruction is more than passing along facts or rules. It is about shaping their souls and forming their character in Christ. Parenting this way means leading with both grace and truth, reflecting how God parents us.

Children's hearts are tender and impressionable. The way we correct, instruct, and model Christlikeness will profoundly shape their understanding of both earthly and heavenly fathers. Parenting driven by anger or control may achieve short-term compliance, but it damages trust and weakens connection.

In contrast, Spirit-led parenting, marked by patience, humility, and encouragement, builds lasting character and deep respect. It lays a foundation of genuine faith that can endure throughout their lives. As fathers, we are called to be intentional, discipling our children in a way that honors God and creates a legacy of blessing for generations to come.

Prayer

Lord, help me to raise my children in a way that reflects Your character and love. Let my correction always be rooted in patience and compassion, and my instruction grounded in grace and truth. Give me wisdom to know when to speak, when to listen, and how to guide their hearts toward You. Shape my parenting so that it points my children to Your kindness, forgiveness, and strength. Help me to model a faith that is real and compelling, so that my children grow to know and trust You deeply. Amen.

Action Step

Make it a priority today to speak life and encouragement over your children. Look for opportunities, especially in moments of correction or discipline, to remind them that their worth is not based on performance or perfection. Speak words that affirm who they are in Christ and let them know you see their effort as much as their mistakes.

As you guide them to grow, anchor your words in love. Let your tone reflect patience and grace, even when firm direction is needed. Remind them often that your love is unwavering and that God's love for them is even greater. In this way, correction becomes not only a lesson but also a chance to strengthen their confidence in the unshakable love of their Father in heaven.

Day 17: Discipline with Love

"For the Lord disciplines the one he loves, and chastises every son whom he receives." Hebrews 12:6–11

Discipline is not punishment. It is discipleship. God corrects us not because He is angry or frustrated, but because He delights in us as His beloved children. In the same way, your role as a father is not to control or break your children's will, but to train and guide them toward maturity in Christ. Loving discipline helps your children understand consequences, embrace responsibility, and develop godly character.

Hebrews reminds us that discipline, though painful in the moment, "yields the peaceful fruit of righteousness" for those who are trained by it. True, loving correction is consistent, calm, and compassionate. It communicates security, not fear.

When discipline is given in love, it builds trust and respect. It provides a safe foundation for growth and maturity. As you discipline with patience and grace, you point your children to the heart of the Father, shaping not only their behavior but also their hearts for a lifetime of faith.

Prayer

Father, thank You for Your loving correction and the patience You show me every day. Help me to discipline my children with that same patience, wisdom, and grace. Let my words guide and train, not tear down or discourage. Give me discernment to know how to balance truth and love, and to correct with a gentle, compassionate spirit. May my discipline always point my children toward Your heart, building them up in confidence and faith. Use me as an instrument of Your nurturing love so that my children grow to know You more deeply through my example. Amen.

Action Step

After you correct your child, take a moment to follow your discipline with words of genuine affirmation. Remind them that correction does not erase love. Speak to their identity, telling them they are loved, valued, and capable of growing. Let them hear that your guidance comes not from anger, but from a desire to see them flourish in character and faith.

Be intentional to make sure discipline always leads your children back to security, not fear. Remind them that your love is steady and that God's love for them is even greater and unshakable. As you balance truth with tenderness, you model the heart of your Heavenly Father, who disciplines those He loves and restores them with grace. This rhythm of correction and affirmation will build trust and anchor them in the safety of love.

Day 18: The Father's Blessing

In the Bible, blessings were never casual well-wishes. They were sacred pronouncements that carried generational weight and spiritual authority. When Isaac blessed Jacob, that moment shaped Jacob's identity, his future, and his legacy. The blessing anchored him in God's promises and gave him strength to endure both struggles and victories.

Speaking blessing should become a rhythm in your home. Bless your children at bedtime, before school, or in moments of fear and uncertainty. Look them in the eye, call them by name, and speak words that affirm their value and call out the good you see in them. Declare God's promises over their future, reminding them that they are chosen, loved, and equipped for His purposes.

A father's words can leave a lasting imprint. Long after your children leave your home, they will carry with them the memory of how you spoke life into their hearts. Make blessing part of your legacy. Let your words guide them with confidence and security as they walk in the purposes of God.

Prayer

God, help me to speak words over my children that shape them in Your truth and love. Let my blessing carry the weight of Your approval, purpose, and steadfast affection. Give me wisdom to see their unique gifts, courage to speak life into their hearts, and faith to declare Your promises over their future. May my words be an anchor for their identity, guiding and strengthening them through every season. Use my voice as an instrument of Your blessing, so my children grow confident in Your love and secure in who You made them to be. Amen.

Action Step

Bless your children today by speaking a specific and heartfelt affirmation to each one. Look them in the eye and call out the good you see in them. Declare God's love over their lives and let them hear that you delight in who they are becoming. These words carry weight and will echo in their hearts long after the moment has passed.

Make blessing a regular rhythm in your home. Just as the patriarchs in Scripture spoke blessings over their children, you can sow seeds of identity, destiny, and hope into the next generation. When your children hear consistent words of life and encouragement, they will learn to see themselves through the lens of God's love and grow in the security of who He has created them to be.

Day 19: Be Present

"And these words that I command you today shall be on your heart. You shall teach them diligently to your children, and shall talk of them when you sit in your house, and when you walk by the way, and when you lie down, and when you rise." – Deuteronomy 6:6–9

Presence outweighs presents. Your children need far more than your provision; they need your presence. Providing financially for your family is important, but it's not enough. Real discipleship and meaningful connection happen not only in big moments but also in the ordinary routines of life.

Being present means more than simply being in the same room. It means giving your full attention. Presence looks like putting away devices, slowing down, and choosing to listen with care. It is engaging in their stories, their questions, and even their struggles. When you show your children that they are seen, heard, and valued, you reflect the love of their Heavenly Father, who delights to be with His children.

The legacy you leave will not be remembered for the material things you provided but for the time and attention you gave. Your children may forget the toys or gifts they received, but they will remember the moments you prayed with them, the evenings you laughed together, and the times you stopped to listen. These daily acts of presence communicate love in its clearest form.

Psalm 127:3 reminds us, *"Children are a heritage from the Lord, the fruit of the womb a reward."* When you invest presence, you honor that heritage. By being intentionally present, you create memories that will anchor your children for years to come, building a legacy that points them to Christ and His unfailing love.

Prayer

Lord, help me to be truly present with my children. Teach me to slow down, set aside distractions, and recognize the holy moments hidden in everyday routines. Let my presence reflect Your love and attention, making my children feel valued, seen, and cherished. Show me how to engage their hearts, listening, guiding, and sharing life together. May the time I spend with them plant seeds of faith, joy, and security that last a lifetime. Thank You for the gift of these moments. Amen.

Action Step

Set aside intentional, device-free time with your children today. Put away phones, turn off screens, and give them the gift of your full attention. Use this opportunity to listen carefully to what is on their hearts, talk honestly about life and faith, and share moments of laughter and joy. Show them that being present with them is more important than anything else competing for your time.

Let this practice become more than an occasional choice. Make it a regular rhythm that reinforces your love and presence as the foundation of your relationship. These simple moments of connection will not only strengthen your bond but also create space for their spiritual growth. In your consistency, your children will see a reflection of their Heavenly Father, who delights to be present with His children.

Day 20: Speak Life

Death and life are in the power of the tongue, and those who love it will eat its fruits." – In God's

---

Words create worlds. The things you say, especially to your wife and children, have the power to breathe life or to sow harm. As a father, your words help shape your children's identity, their confidence, and even their understanding of God's character.

Encouragement should not be rare or reserved for special occasions. It should be woven into the fabric of daily life. Correction and discipline are necessary, but if they are the only words your family hears, they will struggle to see the love behind them. A godly man makes it his habit to build up his wife and children, to celebrate their efforts, and to affirm their worth.

Even when discipline is needed, let your tone and choice of words reflect grace, patience, and purpose. The legacy of your words will endure. Your children will remember how you spoke to them, and your wife will carry the weight of how you honored or dishonored her with your tongue. Choose to speak life daily. Speak words that affirm, bless, and encourage.

When you do, your home will flourish under the blessing of words filled with love and truth, and your family will be strengthened to walk in the confidence of God's grace.

Prayer

Father, help me to speak life into my home. Let my words heal, encourage, and guide with love. Guard my tongue so that everything I say reflects Your heart and builds up those You have entrusted to me. Give me wisdom to use my words to strengthen, comfort, and inspire my family, even in moments of correction. Amen.

Action Step

For every correction you give today, make it a point to follow it with at least two specific words of affirmation or encouragement. Guidance should not end with pointing out what needs to change. It should be balanced by calling out the good you see. Be intentional in noticing your wife's efforts and your children's strengths, and let them hear those things spoken aloud. When you do this, correction is framed not as rejection but as a pathway toward growth and love.

When your words are both truthful and uplifting, they become a source of life and confidence. Your words have the power to shape how your family sees themselves and how they see God. Choose to speak life, so that each member of your household feels valued, loved, and supported. This simple practice will not only soften the weight of correction but will also build a home atmosphere rooted in encouragement, grace, and the steady love of Christ.

Day 21: Model Repentance

"If we confess our sins, he is faithful and just to forgive us our sins and to cleanse us from all unrighteousness." — 1 John 1:9

As a father, you disciple your children not only by what you teach but even more by what you model. Lessons spoken have value, but lessons lived are what sink deep into the heart. When your kids see you humbly acknowledge your wrongs, confess your sins, and walk in the forgiveness of Christ, they learn what real faith and humility look like in daily life.

Your children will make mistakes just as you do. What they need most is not a flawless example but a faithful one. They need to see how to respond when they fall short. If they watch you cover up, justify, or ignore your sins, they may grow to believe that failure is shameful and must be hidden. But if they see you repent openly and receive

By making repentance and grace a normal part of your family customs, you shape your children's view of God. They will come to see Him not as a harsh judge waiting to condemn but as a loving Father who restores and redeems. Every time you admit wrong with humility and extend forgiveness freely, you point your family back to the gospel.

This is the legacy of grace. Your children will not remember you as perfect, but they can remember you as repentant, humble, and anchored in Christ. And in that, they will see the hope and healing that is found in Jesus alone. That is discipleship in its truest form, faith that is real, lived, and daily dependent on the grace of God.

Prayer

Jesus, thank You for Your mercy and the grace You show me each day. Help me to lead my family with true humility, acknowledging my own need for Your forgiveness. Let my example of honest repentance draw my children's hearts closer to You. Give me courage to be open about my struggles and wisdom to point my family to the hope we have in You. May my life reflect the reality of the cross, not just in words, but in how I walk each day. Amen.

Action Step

Share an age-appropriate story with your children about a time when you made a mistake and had to repent. Be honest about what happened but choose a story they can understand without being weighed down by details. Explain how you felt when you failed and how you turned to God for forgiveness. Let them see that even parents stumble and that everyone needs grace.

Then connect your story to the cross. Remind them that Jesus died so our sins could be forgiven and so we could begin again. Show them that God's love is bigger than any failure and that His forgiveness is always available. By sharing your own journey, you point them to Jesus as the true source of hope, healing, and new beginnings. This simple act of transparency can leave a lasting impression on their hearts.

Devotions Week 4:

Finishing Well

A godly life is not measured by a strong start but by a faithful finish. In a world obsessed with quick success and bursts of enthusiasm that fade as quickly as they begin, Scripture calls us to endurance. The Christian walk is not a sprint. It is a marathon, marked by perseverance through trials, setbacks, and long seasons of waiting

Finishing well means staying faithful when no one else sees. It means choosing integrity when compromise would be easier, obedience when popularity pulls in another direction, and purpose when comfort tempts you to coast. Men who leave a lasting legacy are not those who never stumbled, but those who refused to stay down. They rise again and again, rooted in Christ, empowered by the Spirit, and committed to the long road of discipleship

This final week of the Anchored devotional invites you to reflect on your long-term faithfulness in your personal walk with Christ, your family relationships, and your mission in the world. Ask yourself: How will I be remembered? What am I sowing now that will bless generations to come? What kind of legacy will my children and grandchildren inherit from the way I live today? These are not questions of guilt but invitations to intentionality.

God is not looking for perfection. He is looking for perseverance. He delights in the man who presses on, who fights the good fight, who finishes the race, and who keeps the faith to the very end. The reward is not only in the finish line but in the daily faithfulness of running with Christ. Stay anchored. Stay steady. Fix your eyes on Jesus, and let your life tell the story of a man who endured to the end.

Day 22: Run with Endurance

"Therefore, since we are surrounded by so great a cloud of witnesses, let us also lay aside every weight, and sin which clings so closely, and let us run with endurance the race that is set before us" Hebrews 12:1

Faith is not measured by how fast you start but by how you finish. The Christian life is a long journey, marked by seasons of joy, suffering, setbacks, and growth. God does not promise us a trouble-free path, but He does call us to endure. Endurance is the quiet strength to keep going when it would be easier to quit, to stay faithful when the way is hard, and to trust God when the finish line feels far away.

To endure well, we must set aside anything that hinders us. Sometimes these are obvious sins, but other times they are good things that have taken up too much space in our hearts. They weigh us down, sap our energy, and keep us from running with freedom.

Endurance is not about clenching your fists in willpower; it is about opening your hands in surrender. Strength to endure comes not from striving harder but from fixing your eyes on Jesus.

When you keep Him in view, you will find the courage to keep running faithfully until the finish. Paul could say near the end of his life,

"I HAVE FOUGHT THE GOOD FIGHT, I HAVE FINISHED THE RACE, I HAVE KEPT THE FAITH"
2 TIMOTHY 4:7

May the same be true of us. The reward is not just crossing the finish line but finishing with our eyes still fixed on Christ, the One who called us, sustained us, and now waits to welcome us home.

Prayer

Lord, strengthen me to run my race with perseverance and faith. Give me the wisdom to recognize anything that slows me down or distracts me from Your purpose. Help me to let go of every burden or habit that weighs on my heart, and to fix my eyes on You alone. Fill me with endurance for the long journey, and keep my hope anchored in Your promises. May my life bring glory to You as I finish well, relying on Your strength each day. Amen.

Action Step

Take time today to identify one weight or distraction that is slowing your walk with Christ. It may be a habit that drains your focus, a worry that consumes your thoughts, a relationship that pulls you off course, or even a good thing that has taken an unhealthy place in your life. Write it down and bring it honestly before the Lord. Pray with a surrendered heart, asking Him to lift that burden and give you strength to let it go.

Once you lay it down, choose to replace it with something that draws you closer to Jesus. Open His Word and meditate on a passage of Scripture, spend time in worship, or look for a way to serve someone in need. As Hebrews 12:1 reminds us, *"Let us throw off everything that hinders and the sin that so easily entangles. And let us run with perseverance the race marked out for us."* When you release distractions and take hold of practices that feed your soul, you will find new endurance and joy in Christ.

Day 23: Fight the Good Fight

"I have fought the good fight, I have finished the race, I have kept the faith." 2 Timothy 4:7

The Christian life is not a casual stroll. It is a battle, not only against the challenges we see but also against spiritual forces at work in the unseen.

As husbands and fathers, we are engaged in a daily spiritual fight. It is a fight for our integrity in a world that tempts us to compromise. It is a fight for our marriages when our world tells us that commitment is disposable. It is a fight for our children as they are bombarded with lies about their identity and purpose.

Paul reminds us in Ephesians 6:12 that this fight is not against flesh and blood but against rulers, authorities, and spiritual forces of evil. This means the weapons we need are not physical but spiritual. Prayer, God's Word, faith, and the power of the Holy Spirit are our defense and strength. To fight well requires discernment to see the enemy's schemes, courage to stand firm, and perseverance to endure.

To fight the good fight means to pray consistently, even when answers feel delayed. It means to stand for truth in your home, your workplace, and your community, even when it costs you something. It means to love your wife and children with Christlike sacrifice and to model faith that does not quit when trials come.

When your children look back on your life, may they say that you stood firm, that you fought well, and that you lived with faith that endured to the end. That's the victory that glorifies God and leaves a lasting inheritance of hope.

Prayer

God, give me strength to stand firm and courage to fight the battles before me. Help me not to grow weary in doing good, but to persevere with faith and endurance. Remind me that my struggle is not against flesh and blood, but against spiritual forces that seek to undermine my faith and family. Fill me with Your Spirit, so I can finish strong and honor You in every challenge I face. Make me a man who fights for what is right and leads my family with conviction, humility, and love. Amen.

Action Step

Identify one area of struggle in your life today. It may be a personal temptation, a recurring challenge in your marriage, or a heavy burden you carry for your children. Bring it honestly before God in prayer, asking for His wisdom and strength to walk faithfully. Lay it at His feet, trusting that He cares for you and is able to bear what feels too heavy for you alone.

Then take the next step by inviting your wife or a trusted brother in Christ to pray with you. Do not carry the battle in silence.

United prayer brings both accountability and encouragement, reminding you that God has called you into a family of faith. In humility, seek support, and you will find strength you could not muster on your own.

Day 24: Store Up Treasures in Heaven

"Do not lay up for yourselves treasures on earth, where moth and rust destroy and where thieves break in and steal, but lay up for yourselves treasures in heaven..."
Matthew 6:19-20

What you value most will direct the course of your life. Jesus calls us to pursue what truly lasts, seeking eternal treasures rather than temporary rewards. Our earthly achievements, possessions, and recognition all fade with time, but investments made in God's kingdom endure forever.

As a husband and father, you face daily choices that reveal where your treasure truly lies. The way you use your time, energy, and resources shapes not only your own life but also the legacy you pass down. If you give your best to work, hobbies, or status while neglecting the spiritual leadership of your home, your family will see it. If you choose instead to love sacrificially, serve faithfully, and lead spiritually, those choices will bear fruit for generations.

Every decision is an opportunity to invest in what lasts. Faith in Christ, love for your family, integrity in your choices, and service to others are treasures that cannot be taken away. These priorities build a spiritual inheritance that your children and grandchildren will carry with them long after material things have faded.

Choose today to anchor your life in eternal values. Build rhythms of prayer, Scripture, worship, and service into your home. Let your children see what it looks like to put God's kingdom first. By doing so, you leave a legacy of significance that will bless your family and honor the Lord for years to come.

Prayer

Lord, help me to value what You value and to see life through the lens of eternity. Teach me to seek Your kingdom first, choosing eternal rewards over temporary comfort or recognition. Show me how to use my time, resources, and influence to store up treasures that honor You and bless others. Give me wisdom to invest in the things that matter most and courage to let go of what will not last. May my heart be anchored in Your purposes, and my legacy marked by faith, love, and generosity. Amen.

Action Step

Choose one intentional way this week to invest in eternity. Look for an opportunity to serve someone in need, give sacrificially, or come alongside a younger believer who needs encouragement. It does not have to be dramatic or complicated. Every choice to love, serve, and give in His name carries eternal weight.

Set aside time or resources with a willing heart, remembering that faithfulness is what God values most. A simple phone call to encourage someone, a meal shared with a neighbor, or a quiet act of generosity may seem small in the moment, but heaven measures it differently.

Make a deliberate choice to focus not on what is temporary but on what will last forever. Earthly recognition fades, but eternal treasure endures. When you live with eternity in view, your life becomes a testimony of hope. Your family and those around you will see in your choices that Christ is your treasure, and your legacy will point them toward Him.

Day 25: Remain Faithful

"Be faithful unto death, and I will give you the crown of life." – *Revelation 2:10*

Faithfulness is rarely glamorous. It does not draw the spotlight or attract the applause of crowds, yet in the eyes of God, it is one of the most valuable qualities a man can possess. To remain faithful means showing up day after day, for your marriage, your children, your calling, and your walk with the Lord. It is the quiet choice to keep loving, keep serving, and keep trusting, even when the feelings fade or the path feels uncertain.

In a culture that prizes quick success and celebrates easy exits, steady commitment shines like a light in the darkness. The world may honor talent, charisma, or wealth, but God looks for men who are consistent, steadfast, and dependable

Faithfulness is built in the small rhythms of perseverance: praying when you would rather sleep, showing kindness when you feel overlooked, serving your family even when you are tired. These acts may not seem like much, but they are bricks in a foundation that can withstand storms. When challenges come, the man who has cultivated daily faithfulness will remain standing, anchored in Christ.

Let your faithfulness be a living testimony to your family and to the world. Show them that the enduring power of a life anchored in Christ is worth more than fleeting success. Your steadfastness will become part of your legacy, pointing those who watch you to the faithfulness of the God you serve.

Prayer

Jesus, help me to remain faithful through every season, whether in times of joy or difficulty. Strengthen me when I feel weary and give me courage to keep going when I am tempted to give up. Teach me to live for Your approval alone, not for the praise or recognition of others. Remind me daily that You are worth every sacrifice and that my faithfulness matters to You. Let my life be marked by steadfast love and unwavering commitment, bringing honor to Your name. Amen.

Action Step

There is power in putting words to your commitments. Writing a declaration is more than jotting down nice thoughts. It is an act of aligning your heart, your priorities, and your mission with the calling God has placed on your life.

Take time today to write down a short declaration of commitment to God and to your family. Keep it simple but heartfelt, something that captures the mission you desire to live out daily. Choose words that resonate deeply with your own journey and convictions.

Post your declaration somewhere you will see it often, such as on your mirror, your desk, or your nightstand. Each time you read it, let it remind you of your identity in Christ and the mission He has entrusted to you. Over time, these words will sink into your heart and strengthen your resolve to live faithfully. When you are tired, they will call you to endurance. When you are distracted, they will call you back to focus.

This simple step of writing and displaying your declaration can become a powerful anchor for your life and legacy. Let it guide your choices and fuel your perseverance. In doing so, you not only keep your own steps steady but also leave behind a visible testimony for your family of what it looks like to walk faithfully with God.

Day 26: Keep the Word Before You

"Your word is a lamp to my feet and a light to my path." – Psalm 119:105

In a dark and confusing world, God's Word is our lamp. It shines into the chaos and shows us the way when everything else feels uncertain. As husbands and fathers, we are not called to lead by guesswork or by following the shifting voices of society. We are called to guide with conviction, rooted in the steady truth of Scripture.

Reading God's Word daily is not just a discipline for the spiritually mature; it is essential for survival. Just as our bodies cannot go long without food, our souls cannot thrive without the bread of life. When we store God's Word in our hearts, it shapes our thoughts, tempers our responses, and strengthens our faith in the battles we face each day.

Let the Bible be your compass. Allow it to correct you when you are wrong, comfort you in sorrow, and call you higher in every area of life. Let your children see you reading it, hear you quoting it, and know that you treasure it. In doing so, you model for them that the Word of God is not distant or abstract, but a living guide for daily life.

There is no substitute for the steady and transforming influence of Scripture. Every verse you hide in your heart, every truth you teach to your family, every decision you align with God's Word is shaping a legacy that will outlast you. Scripture is the anchor that will set the direction of your family for generations to come.

Prayer

Father, let Your Word be the guiding light of my life. Shape my thoughts, decisions, and actions by the truth of Scripture. May my home be filled with Your Word and my heart rooted in its promises. Help me to treasure and live out Your truth each day. Amen.

Action Step

Choose one verse to memorize today and make it your focus. Write it on a card, a sticky note, or save it on your phone, and carry it with you wherever you go. Read it in the morning, review it during breaks, and repeat it silently as you work or drive.

Memorizing Scripture is more than an exercise of the mind, it is food for the soul. When the Word takes root in you, it shapes your thoughts, guides your speech, and strengthens your faith in everyday battles. The Spirit will bring those verses to your mind when you need them most, whether in a moment of temptation, a time of fear, or a chance to encourage someone else.

Before the day ends, share the verse you've memorized with someone close to you. Tell your wife, your children, or a friend what it means to you and how it is shaping your thoughts. This simple act turns Scripture into a living influence, not only in your own heart but also in your home and relationships.

There is no substitute for the steady impact of hiding God's Word in your heart. Each verse you commit to memory is a seed planted that will bear fruit in due time. Over weeks and months, those seeds grow into a storehouse of truth that will guide you through every season of life. Begin today with one verse. Let God's truth dwell richly in you, and watch how it transforms not only your life but also the lives of those around you.

Day 27: Leave a Spiritual Inheritance

"A good man leaves an inheritance to his children's children, but the sinner's wealth is laid up for the righteous." – Proverbs 13:22

True inheritance goes far beyond finances. As a godly father or grandfather, your legacy is measured not in what you accumulate but in the spiritual seeds you plant within your family. The psalmist declares,

> *"A GOOD MAN LEAVES AN INHERITANCE TO HIS CHILDREN'S CHILDREN"*
> *PROVERBS 13:22*

That inheritance is not only material provision but also the gift of a life rooted in Christ.

When you consistently model a life of prayer, truth, integrity, and love for Jesus, you leave behind something the world cannot steal or diminish. Your children and grandchildren may forget the gifts you purchased for them, but they will not forget hearing you pray aloud, watching you read God's Word, or seeing you choose righteousness when compromise was easier. Those quiet, faithful choices shape their vision of what it means to walk with God.

Ask yourself: What spiritual memories will your family carry with them? Will they remember that you spoke blessing over them, encouraged them in their struggles, and treated others with compassion? Will they recall moments when you admitted your mistakes, asked forgiveness, and modeled repentance? The influence you pass on is found not only in what you provide but in how you live day by day.

Prayer

God, make my life a blessing for those who come after me. Help me pass on more than wisdom or advice, help me pass on a living, active faith that is rooted in Your love and promises. Let my children and grandchildren come to know You personally because of the life I lived before them. Shape my words, actions, and example so that they point the next generation to Christ. May my legacy be one of faithfulness, hope, and trust in You. Amen.

Action Step

Take intentional time this week to write a letter of spiritual encouragement to your children or grandchildren. In your own words, share a part of your faith journey. It might be a lesson you learned through struggle, a moment when God's grace carried you, or a testimony of His faithfulness in a difficult season. Be honest about your imperfections so they see your walk with God is real and rooted in His mercy, not in your strength. Your transparency will give them courage in their own walk of faith.

In your letter, affirm their worth and identity in Christ. Remind them that they are loved not for what they accomplish but because they belong to God. Choose words that breathe encouragement, faith, and love, so that every time they return to your letter, they feel strengthened by your voice and by God's Word.

Do not underestimate the power of written words. Long after conversations are forgotten, a letter can remain, tucked away and reread in times of need. Just as Paul wrote letters of encouragement to his spiritual children, you can do the same for those entrusted to your care. In doing so, you leave behind not only memories, but a legacy of faith that will continue to speak long after you are gone.

Day 28: Walk in the Spirit

So I say, walk by the Spirit, and you will not gratify the desires of the flesh. For the flesh desires what is contrary to the Spirit, and the Spirit what is contrary to the flesh. They are in conflict with each other, so that you are not to do whatever you want. – Galatians 5:16–18

The Christian life is not meant to be lived by sheer willpower or self-effort. No amount of determination or discipline can produce true transformation. God graciously gives us His Spirit to guide, empower, and reshape us from the inside out. As a husband and father, your family needs more than your best intentions or promises to do better. What they need is to see the evidence of the Holy Spirit alive in you, bearing fruit that human effort could never produce.

Every time you choose patience instead of anger, kindness instead of selfishness, or joy in the midst of stress, you are showing your family a picture of Jesus. These moments may seem small, but they leave lasting impressions. Children learn what love looks like when they see it practiced in the home. Wives are encouraged and strengthened when they experience grace flowing from their husband. The Spirit's work in you is not only for your own maturity but also for the blessing, encouragement, and shaping of those who are closest to you.

Relying on the Holy Spirit each day frees you from the burden of trying to lead in your own strength. It allows you to love with a love that goes beyond your limits, to serve with humility that does not come naturally, and to lead with wisdom that is not your own. When you live in step with the Spirit, you leave behind a legacy far greater than words or intentions. You leave a pattern of faith and Christlike character that points your family directly to the power of God alive within you.

Prayer

Holy Spirit, lead me today and fill my life with Your presence. Help me to walk by Your power, not my own strength or desires. Grow Your fruit in my heart, love, joy, peace, patience, kindness, goodness, faithfulness, gentleness, and self-control, so that my family sees more of Christ in me every day. Teach me to surrender, listen, and obey Your voice in both the big and small moments. Make my home a place where Your Spirit is evident and Your love flows freely. Amen.

Action Step

Gather your family together this evening and ask them two simple but powerful questions: *"Which fruit of the Spirit do you see most in me? Which one do you think I need to grow in?"* These questions may feel vulnerable, but they open the door to honest reflection and deeper connection. When you ask with humility, you show your family that growth in Christ is a lifelong journey for every believer, including you.

Listen carefully to their answers without defensiveness. Resist the urge to explain yourself or push back. Instead, receive their words with gratitude, even if they are difficult to hear. Remember that God often speaks to us through the voices of those closest to us. Honest feedback is not an attack; it is one of the ways God shapes us into Christlikeness. Your willingness to listen sets an example for your family of what true humility looks like.

Use what they share to guide your prayers and your focus for intentional growth. If they affirm patience in you, thank God for cultivating that fruit. If they point out a lack of gentleness or self-control, bring it to the Lord and ask Him to make you stronger in that area. This is not about striving in your own strength but about yielding more fully to the Spirit.

Devotions Bonus Weekend:

Commissioned

This final weekend devotion marks the transition from formation to mission. After anchoring your identity in Christ, strengthening your marriage, and leading your children intentionally, the call now is to go. You are not just a man of faith behind closed doors; you are a disciple sent into the world with purpose. Just as Jesus commissioned His followers in Matthew 28:19–20, He sends you with the same authority and power: to make disciples, to lead boldly, and to live faithfully.

Being commissioned means you carry the presence and mission of Christ into every space, your home, your workplace, your community, and beyond. You are called to be strong and courageous, not because of your strength, but because the Lord goes with you.

This weekend, pause and reflect on the work God has done in you. Think about the past 28 days. Let it stir both gratitude and resolve. Our world needs men who stand firm in Christ. Men who love deeply. Men who lead with humility and strength.

You were made for this moment. Now, go live it.

You are commissioned!

Day 29: Be Strong and Courageous

Have I not commanded you? Be strong and courageous. Do not be frightened, and do not be dismayed, for the Lord your God is with you wherever you go." — Joshua 1:9

This is an invitation to dependence. Strength and courage in the biblical sense are not rooted in personality, talent, or grit; they are rooted in God's abiding presence.

As husbands and fathers, we will all face moments when fear grips us, when pressure feels overwhelming, or when the path ahead is clouded with uncertainty. Sometimes it comes in the form of a difficult financial season, a child making painful choices, or a marriage stretched thin under the weight of stress. In those moments, courage does not mean pretending we aren't afraid. Courage is choosing to step forward in faith even when fear is still whispering in our ear.

The good news is this: the same God who stood with Joshua on the banks of the Jordan stands with us in the storms of life. He does not promise us a path free from hardship, but He does promise

That is why courage, for the man of God, is not bravado or self-reliance. It is surrender. It is saying, *"Lord, I cannot do this in my own strength, but I know You go before me."* When we lean into Him, we find the power to keep leading even when we feel inadequate, the faith to keep praying even when we can't see the outcome, and the love to keep serving even when we feel empty.

Joshua's call is our call: to lead with courage that comes not from ourselves but from the unshakable presence of God.

Prayer

Lord, thank You for always being with me. I confess that fear sometimes causes me to hesitate or shrink back. Help me to trust You fully and to lead my family with steadfastness and integrity that comes from Your presence. Remind me daily that I never walk alone, and that Your power is made perfect in my weakness. Fill my heart with faith to follow wherever You lead and let my life be a testimony of Your faithfulness and love. Amen.

Action Step

Take a bold step of obedience this weekend in an area where you know God is prompting you. It may be spiritual, such as beginning a new rhythm of prayer or Scripture reading. It may be relational, such as starting a conversation you have been avoiding or choosing forgiveness where bitterness has taken root. It may even be practical, like committing to gathering your family for worship or setting aside time to serve someone in need. Do not wait for the perfect moment. Choose to act in faith, believing that God honors even the small steps of obedience.

As you move forward, trust God to supply the courage you need. Pray for His strength and lean on His promises. Remember the words given to Joshua: "Be strong and courageous. Do not be afraid; do not be discouraged, for the Lord your God will be with you wherever you go". Each act of obedience is not only a step of faith for you but also an act of leadership for those watching your life. When you lead your family with boldness rooted in Christ, you give them a living example of what it means to follow Him with courage and conviction.

Day 30: Go and Make Disciples

Go therefore and make disciples of all nations, baptizing them in the name of the Father and of the Son and of the Holy Spirit, 20 teaching them to observe all that I have commanded you. And behold, I am with you always, to the end of the age." – Matthew 28:19–20

The Great Commission was never meant only for pastors or missionaries. When Jesus said, "Go and make disciples of all nations", He was speaking to every believer. That calling begins in the home.

As a husband, your first mission is to love your wife as Christ loved the church. That love is discipleship in action, teaching by example what covenant faithfulness looks like. As a father, your mission is to disciple your children by pointing them toward Christ in your words, habits, and choices. Each prayer, each meal shared with gratitude, each act of loving discipline is a chance to shape their hearts for God.

Your mission, however, does not stop at home. God's call extends into every sphere of life. Your coworkers notice how you handle pressure. Your neighbors see how you treat your family. Your friends observe whether your faith is consistent in both private and public. Even small routines and conversations can become testimonies of the gospel.

You may never preach to thousands or travel across the world, but you have been placed exactly where you are for a reason. Your home, your workplace, and your community are your mission field. Be faithful there, and your influence will ripple outward in ways you may never fully see.

Prayer

Jesus, thank You for trusting me with Your mission and for giving me the privilege of representing You wherever I go. Send me as Your ambassador into every space I enter, beginning with my home and extending to my workplace, neighborhood, and beyond. Help me to lead, love, and disciple in a way that points others to You. Fill me with boldness, wisdom, and compassion so that my life reflects Your heart and draws others closer to You. Amen.

Action Step

Identify one person outside your immediate family whom you can disciple or encourage in Christ. Pray for them by name, asking God to open doors for meaningful connection. Consider a neighbor, coworker, friend, or younger believer who may need guidance or encouragement. Discipleship does not always begin with a formal study. Often it starts with simple presence, care, and prayerful attention.

Take a step this week to reach out. Initiate a genuine conversation, send an encouraging message, or invite them into a spiritual gathering or time of prayer. Be intentional about weaving discipleship into your everyday relationships, remembering Jesus' command in Matthew 28:19: "Go therefore and make disciples of all nations." As you invest in others with humility and faith, God will use your obedience to shape lives for His kingdom.

Do not underestimate the small steps. A kind word can soften a heart. A simple prayer can open the door to deeper conversations. An invitation to share a meal can become the beginning of a mentoring relationship. God delights to use ordinary acts of faithfulness to accomplish extraordinary purposes, and He will honor your willingness to make yourself available.

Group Study Guide

This guide is designed to facilitate meaningful group discussion, reflection, and accountability through the 30-day "*Anchored*" devotional for husbands and fathers. Whether you're meeting with a group of men in your church, a few trusted friends, or your small group, these sessions are crafted to help deepen your understanding, sharpen your faith, and strengthen your role as a spiritual leader.

Each week focuses on a foundational theme: Identity in Christ, Anchored in Marriage, Intentional Fatherhood, and Finishing Well. For each theme, the guide includes a summary, a set of thought-provoking group discussion questions, and a weekly Scripture memory verse. These components are designed to help internalize biblical truths and apply them practically in your marriage, family, and leadership.

This guide isn't just for study, it's for transformation. As you walk this journey together, may you grow in Christ, sharpen one another, and become anchored men who impact generations.

Session 1: Foundations of Identity

Every man leads from the core of who he believes himself to be. If you see yourself through the lens of failure, shame, or insecurity, your leadership will reflect fear and self-protection. But when you see yourself through the truth of Scripture, as a son of God and a new creation in Christ, your leadership becomes rooted in confidence, humility, and love.

When you step into marriage and fatherhood with this mindset, everything changes. Being a new creation means you do not have to repeat the broken patterns of your past. It means you can lead your home with courage instead of fear, with service instead of pride, and with grace instead of harshness. Your wife and children need more than a man who provides; they need a man who knows who he is in Christ and leads them from that place of security and faith.

Discussion Questions:

- Which identity truth from this week hit you most personally?
- How have you been tempted to find identity in performance instead of Christ?
- What does being a "new creation" mean practically for your marriage and fatherhood?

Memory Verse: 2 Corinthians 5:17

Session 2: Anchored in Marriage

Marriage was never meant to be a human invention. It is God's design, created to be a living picture of Christ's love for His Church. When husbands and wives walk in unity and love, their relationship points to the gospel itself. This makes marriage more than companionship, it is a calling and a testimony.

When a husband takes this calling seriously, his love becomes a sermon his family sees daily. His children learn what Christ's love looks like in action. His wife is built up, strengthened, and secured in the knowledge that she is loved. And the world around them catches a glimpse of the gospel through their covenant love.

Discussion Questions:

- What does it look like to love your wife as Christ loved the Church?

- What practical barriers stand in the way of spiritual unity in your marriage?

- How are you honoring and cherishing your wife with your words and actions?

Memory Verse: Ephesians 5:25

Session 3: Intentional Fatherhood

The first and most important place where discipleship happens is not in the church building but around the dinner table, during bedtime prayers, and in everyday conversations. As fathers, we are called to be the spiritual leaders of our homes, showing our children what it means to follow Christ not only with words, but with consistent actions.

When discipleship is woven into the fabric of family life, our homes become the training ground for future generations of faith. Our children learn who God is not only from what we teach but from how we live.

Discussion Questions:

- In what ways are you discipling your children daily?
- What does loving discipline look like in your home?
- How do you model repentance and grace to your children?

Memory Verse: Ephesians 6:4

Session 4: Finishing Well

A godly legacy does not happen by accident. It is the fruit of daily choices to walk with Christ, to obey His Word, and to endure through challenges with faith. The greatest inheritance we can leave our families is not wealth or possessions, but the example of a life faithfully lived for the glory of God.

The apostle Paul reflects on his own legacy in 2 Timothy 4:7: *"I have fought the good fight, I have finished the race, I have kept the faith."* His confidence came not from a perfect life, but from a faithful life. Obedience in the small things, perseverance through trials, and trust in God's promises prepared him to finish well. That same endurance is what builds a legacy that outlives us.

Legacy is not about grand gestures, but about consistent obedience and endurance. The way you choose to walk with Christ today will echo for generations to come.

Discussion Questions:

- What distractions or sins are keeping you from running with endurance?
- How are you intentionally leaving a spiritual inheritance?
- Who are your spiritual encouragers and accountability partners?

Memory Verse: Hebrews 12:1–2

Bonus Session: Commissioned

God has entrusted you with the sacred responsibility of leading your home. Your wife and children are your first disciples, and your daily faithfulness is one of the greatest testimonies of the gospel. Yet the call of Christ does not stop at your front door. A godly man leads both in his household and beyond it, stepping into the world as a witness for Jesus.

Jesus expands this vision in Matthew 28:19–20: *"Go therefore and make disciples of all nations… teaching them to observe all that I have commanded you. And behold, I am with you always, to the end of the age."* Every man of God is called to live with this Great Commission in mind. Your mission may begin with your family, but it extends to neighbors, coworkers, friends, and even the next generation of men who need encouragement and example.

Living this out does not require a stage or a spotlight. It requires presence, intentionality, and obedience. Discipleship happens in everyday conversations, in acts of service, in shared prayers, and in the willingness to speak the name of Jesus with boldness. The legacy of your home becomes the launching point for impact in your community and beyond.

Discussion Questions:

- Where is God calling you to lead boldly?
- Who in your life can you begin to disciple?
- How can this group continue to encourage one another beyond these 30 days?

Commissioning Challenge: Pray over one another. Speak life, identity, and purpose. Commit to go and make disciples in your homes and beyond.

DEVOTINAL COMPANION
Five Daily Habits to Build

To become the godly man, husband, and Father God calls you to be, it's essential to cultivate spiritual disciplines that anchor your life in Christ. This isn't about rigid legalism, but about a vibrant, transformative relationship with your Creator. Here are five foundational pillars to build upon:

Daily Surrender

The pull to launch into your day already consumed by the world is strong. Before your head has cleared, the phone beckons, social media feeds, market reports, breaking news, the ever-growing stack of emails. Without realizing it, you've bowed to the world before you've bowed to God.

But Scripture calls us to a better way. The first moments of the day set the course of the heart. Instead of rushing into noise, cultivate the discipline of surrender. Before your feet touch the floor, or certainly before your thumbs touch a screen, whisper a prayer of dependence: *"Father, I cannot do this without You. Fill me. Lead me. Use me."*

This is not empty ritual. It is a declaration of reality. You are not sufficient in yourself. You are in desperate need of the Spirit's wisdom, strength, and guidance. That prayer is your anchor. It aligns your heart with heaven before you face the earth.

In that simple act of surrender, the compass of your soul is reset. Your day begins not in your own strength, but in God's. Not chasing your own plans but walking in His.

Scripture Saturation

The way your body cannot thrive without daily nourishment, your soul cannot flourish apart from the living Word of God

Notice, *richly,* not sparingly. This is not a call for a quick glance or a box to check, but for Scripture to take up residence in you, to soak into every part of your life.

That doesn't mean you need hours each morning. Even ten minutes of focused, undistracted time can reshape your entire day. Read slowly. Pause. Ask simple but piercing questions: *"Lord, what are You saying to me here? How does this truth touch my life today?"*

When you do this constantly, those ten minutes will begin to *"tilt your whole day."* God's Word recalibrates your perspective, renews your mind, and arms you against the pull of temptation. Over time, this daily immersion is not about information, it is about transformation.

Rich saturation in Scripture is a journey. Each day adds another layer, another insight, another step of growth. The Word not only feeds you; it forms you.

Regular Confession

Sin, left unaddressed, can grieve the Holy Spirit and erect barriers in your relationship with Ephesians 4:30 gives us a sobering reminder: *"Do not grieve the Holy Spirit of God."* This isn't meant to press believers under a burden of constant condemnation, but to call us into a tender, honest, ongoing relationship with our father.

One of the simplest yet most powerful ways to walk in step with the Spirit is through regular confession, keeping what older saints have called a *"short account with God."* When you sense sin in your heart, whether it's a stray thought, a sharp word, or a selfish choice, bring it to Him swiftly. Don't let it sit. Left unconfessed, sin is like plague on the soul, hardening the heart and dulling your spiritual sensitivity.

But confession clears the clog. It brings forgiveness, restores intimacy, and keeps your heart tender. Each time you repent, you acknowledge God's holiness and your daily dependence on His grace. This rhythm of self-examination and quick repentance trains the heart to stay soft, eager to obey, and sensitive to the Spirit's leading.

Brotherhood

The Christian life was never designed to be walked alone. Lone-ranger Christianity is not only unbiblical, but also dangerous.

You need brothers in Christ, men who love you enough to tell you the truth, even when it stings. Men who will ask the hard questions that pierce through your excuses. Men who will pray with you, fight for you, and hold you steady when the storms come. Isolation may feel easier, but it's spiritual suicide. A man cut off from fellowship is a man exposed to the enemy's schemes, with no accountability and no encouragement to keep him standing.

That's why you must purposefully seek out godly friendships. Invest in a band of brothers who will sharpen your faith, call out your blind spots, and celebrate your victories. A true brotherhood isn't a luxury, it's a lifeline. In the battles of life, every man needs a foxhole filled with faithful men who have his back.

Rest and Silence

In our hyper-connected, noisy world, the discipline of rest and silence feels counter-intuitive, yet it is profoundly spiritual. It is in the quiet places that the Spirit's voice becomes clear.

But quiet doesn't come naturally. ESPN blares the scores, your inbox won't stop filling, and political arguments echo from every corner of the internet. All of it can drown out the gentle whispers of God. That's why you must deliberately *turn it off* and *shut it down*.

Rest is not neglecting responsibility; it is creating sacred space. Space to breathe. Space to pray without words. Space simply to be in His presence. In those holy pockets of silence, God restores what the noise has drained. He speaks with clarity. He steadies your heart. He renews your perspective.

Silence is not empty; it is full of God